From Peer to Leader

Mastering the Shift to Management

Heather Wampler

Copyright ©2024 by Heather Wampler. All rights reserved.

No part of this publication may be reproduced, distributed, or transmitted in any form or by any means, including photocopying, recording, or other electronic or mechanical methods, without the prior written permission of the publisher, except in the case of brief quotations embodied in critical reviews and certain other noncommercial uses permitted by copyright law.

For permission requests, please contact the author.

This book is intended as a reference guide and is based on the author's experiences and research. The author and publisher have made every effort to ensure the accuracy and completeness of the information herein and cannot accept any legal responsibility for any errors or omissions or for any consequences resulting from the use of the information contained in this book.

First edition: 2024

Table of Contents

Index   **1**

Acknowledgment   4

Introduction: Becoming the Leader You Were Meant to Be   5

Chapter 1: You've Earned It: Accepting Your New Role   **7**

Chapter 2: Rewiring Relationships: From Peer to Leader   **15**

Chapter 3: Your Leadership Persona: Discovering Your Management Style   23

Chapter 4: Adopting a Leader's Mindset   31

Chapter 5: Communication is Key: Leading Through Words   37

Chapter 6: Delegation 101: Letting Go Without Losing Control   48

Chapter 7: The Feedback Formula: Giving and Receiving Input   55

Chapter 8: Managing Conflict: Turning Tension into Collaboration   61

Chapter 9: Managing Up: Building Strong Relationships with Your Boss   77

Chapter 10: Time Management for Leaders: Balancing Priorities in a Demanding Role   85

Chapter 11: Emotional Intelligence in Leadership: Leading with Empathy and Awareness   92

Chapter 12: Decision-Making in Leadership: Balancing Logic and Intuition   99

Chapter 13: Building a High-Performance Team:
Unlocking Potential and Driving Results 106
Chapter 15: Sustaining Leadership Growth: A
Commitment to Continuous Improvement 119
Chapter 16: Leaving a Legacy: The Impact of Great
Leadership 125
Conclusion: The Leadership Journey **134**
Index **141**

Index

Part 1: The Transition to Leadership

1. **From Peer to Leader**
   - Understanding the Challenges of Leadership
   - Navigating Role Changes
   - Establishing Authority Without Alienating
   - Building Trust and Credibility
2. **Strengthening Relationships in Leadership**
   - Shifting Dynamics with Former Peers
   - Cultivating Professional Boundaries
   - Strengthening New Relationships
   - Leading with Empathy
3. **Understanding Leadership Styles**
   - Common Leadership Styles
   - Discovering Your Leadership Style
   - Adapting Your Style to Your Team's Needs
   - The Role of Flexibility in Leadership

4. **Managing Up**
   - Building a Strong Relationship with Your Boss
   - Communicating Upward Effectively
   - Anticipating Needs and Prioritizing Goals
   - Navigating Misalignment and Conflict

Part 2: Skills for Effective Leadership

5. **Time Management for Leaders**
   - Balancing Priorities in a Demanding Role
   - Delegation as a Time-Management Tool
   - Strategic Planning and Focus
   - Avoiding Burnout as a Leader

6. **Decision-Making in Leadership**
   - The Role of Logic and Intuition
   - Making Decisions Under Pressure
   - Engaging the Team in Decisions
   - Owning Outcomes and Learning from Mistakes

7. **Emotional Intelligence in Leadership**
   - The Five Pillars of Emotional Intelligence
   - Managing Emotions Effectively

- Building Stronger Relationships with Empathy
- Handling Emotional Conflict in the Workplace

Part 3: Building High-Performing Teams

8. **Building a High-Performance Team**
    - Characteristics of Successful Teams
    - Hiring and Onboarding for Success
    - Building Trust and Accountability
    - Sustaining Team Growth and Performance

9. **Leading Through Change**
    - The Emotional Impact of Change on Teams
    - Communicating Change Effectively
    - Leading with Empathy in Uncertain Times
    - Building Resilience and Adaptability

Part 4: Legacy and Leadership Longevity

10. **Sustaining Leadership Growth**
    - Embracing a Growth Mindset
    - Seeking Feedback for Improvement
    - Balancing Personal Development with Team Needs
    - Staying Resilient and Adaptable
11. **Leaving a Leadership Legacy**
    - Defining the Legacy You Want to Leave
    - Building a Culture That Outlasts You
    - Mentoring and Developing Future Leaders
    - Aligning Your Daily Actions with Your Long-Term Impact

Acknowledgment

To my husband, the love of my life and my greatest supporter.

Your unwavering belief in me has been the foundation of everything I've accomplished. In moments of doubt, you've been my anchor. In moments of triumph, you've been my biggest cheerleader. Your love, patience, and encouragement have given me the strength to take on challenges I never thought I could face and to become the person—and the leader—I am today.

This book exists because of you. Your quiet strength, thoughtful advice, and endless support have been my guiding light. You've taught me the power of love and partnership, and for that, I am endlessly grateful.

Every word in these pages is inspired by your belief in me, and every success I've achieved is a reflection of the life we've built together. Thank you for being my heart, my home, and my forever partner in this beautiful journey of life.

Introduction: Becoming the Leader You Were Meant to Be

Leadership is a calling. Whether you've stepped into a leadership role for the first time or you've been leading for years, you've answered the call to guide, inspire, and shape the world around you. This decision is not just about achieving goals or climbing the ranks—it's about making an impact that resonates far beyond yourself.

Leadership is one of the most challenging and rewarding journeys you'll ever take. It's a path filled with tough decisions, uncertain moments, and opportunities to rise to the occasion. It's about learning to balance authority with empathy, results with relationships, and ambition with humility. Most importantly, it's about embracing the opportunity to lift others up, helping them achieve more than they ever thought possible.

This book is your guide to navigating the complexities of leadership. It's for anyone who's ever struggled with the challenges of stepping into a management role, questioned their ability to inspire others, or wondered how to leave a lasting mark as a leader. It's not just about tools and strategies—it's about mindset, values, and the commitment to grow continuously.

Inside, you'll find practical advice, actionable steps, and thought-provoking insights that will help you:

- Transition into leadership with confidence and clarity.
- Build trust, inspire loyalty, and create high-performing teams.
- Master the art of decision-making, emotional intelligence, and leading through change.
- Cultivate a legacy that endures long after you've moved on.

But this book is also an invitation—to reflect on the kind of leader you want to be. Leadership isn't one-size-fits-all. It's deeply personal, shaped by your values, experiences, and aspirations. My hope is that as you move through these pages, you'll find the clarity, inspiration, and courage to step fully into your potential as a leader.

Remember: Leadership is not about perfection—it's about progress. It's about having the humility to learn, the resilience to adapt, and the heart to make a difference. Your leadership matters more than you realize, and the journey you're on is one of the most important you'll ever take.

Let's begin the journey together.

Chapter 1: You've Earned It: Accepting Your New Role

Introduction: From Peer to Leader

Imagine this: It's your first day as a manager. You walk into the office (or log onto your first meeting), and everything feels familiar—the workspace, the faces, the flow of the day. But something is different. People look to you now, not as a colleague or equal, but as their leader.

The shift can be exhilarating, but also intimidating. Yesterday, your job was to focus on your own tasks and goals. Today, you're responsible for an entire group of people—their productivity, morale, and growth are now part of your job description. It's no longer just about what you accomplish, but about what your team accomplishes under your guidance.

This transition, from individual contributor to leader, is one of the most significant changes you'll experience in your career. And while it's a tremendous opportunity, it's also fraught with challenges.

Let's get one thing out of the way: **No one feels 100% ready to be a manager on Day One.** Even seasoned leaders admit that their first time stepping into a leadership role was full of uncertainty and self-doubt. That's because leadership isn't about being perfect; it's about learning, adapting, and growing alongside your team.

Why the Peer-to-Leader Transition is Unique

Becoming a manager is challenging for anyone, but the transition is especially tricky when you're managing people who used to be your peers. Yesterday, you were part of the team, cracking jokes in the breakroom and commiserating over tight deadlines. Today, you're the one setting those deadlines, giving feedback, and holding people accountable.

The dynamics have shifted, and that shift can create a sense of awkwardness—for you and for them. You may worry about losing friendships or being seen as "one of us turned into one of them." Your team may question how things will change now that you're in charge.

These concerns are valid, but here's the good news: You're not alone in facing them. Many first-time managers have successfully navigated this exact situation, and you can too. The key lies in **understanding the unique challenges of this transition and developing the skills to overcome them.**

The Emotional Rollercoaster of Leadership

Stepping into leadership often feels like a mix of excitement and anxiety. On one hand, you feel proud that your hard work and contributions have been recognized. You're ready to take on this new challenge and prove yourself in a bigger role.

On the other hand, you may feel overwhelmed by questions like:

- *"Am I really ready for this?"*
- *"How do I manage people who are older or more experienced than me?"*
- *"What if I fail?"*

These emotions are completely normal. Leadership brings uncertainty, but it also brings opportunity—the opportunity to make an impact not just through your own work, but through the success of others.

Here's the truth: You wouldn't be in this role if people didn't believe you could handle it. Your leaders saw something in you—your skills, your attitude, your ability to inspire others—and they trust you to succeed.

Now, it's time for you to believe in yourself.

Your First Day as a Manager: What to Expect

The first day in any new role comes with a mix of excitement and unease, but moving into management adds an extra layer of complexity. You may feel the pressure to make a strong impression or to establish yourself as a capable leader right away.

But here's the thing: Your first day isn't about solving every problem or proving yourself. It's about **listening, observing, and setting the tone**.

What does that look like in practice?

- **Listening to Your Team**: Schedule time to talk with your team members individually. Learn about their goals, challenges, and concerns.
- **Observing the Dynamics**: Pay attention to how the team operates. Are there any unspoken rules, power dynamics, or tensions that need addressing?
- **Setting the Tone**: From Day One, your actions set the standard for how you'll lead. Be approachable, curious, and clear about your intentions.

Remember, leadership is a marathon, not a sprint. Your first day is just the beginning of a journey that will require patience, adaptability, and a willingness to learn.

Leadership is About Growth, Not Perfection

One of the biggest misconceptions about leadership is that you need to have all the answers. Many new managers put immense pressure on themselves to be perfect, thinking they need to know everything right away.

But here's the reality: **Leadership isn't about perfection—it's about growth.**

Great leaders are learners. They seek feedback, admit their mistakes, and continually improve. They understand that leadership isn't a destination; it's a journey. And like any journey, it will have its ups and downs.

So, as you step into this new role, give yourself permission to learn and grow. You're not expected to know everything on Day One, and that's okay. What matters is your commitment to becoming the best leader you can be—for yourself, for your team, and for your organization.

A Personal Story to Inspire You

Let's look at the story of Megan, a new manager who faced many of the same fears and challenges you might be feeling.

Megan was promoted after five years as a high-performing software engineer. She was excited but nervous—her new team included several people she'd worked alongside for years, and one person who had even mentored her when she first joined the company. She worried about how they'd react to her promotion.

Her first day was tough. Megan overcompensated by trying to show she was "in charge," micromanaging tasks and avoiding casual conversations with her team. This created tension—her team felt like she didn't trust them, and Megan felt increasingly isolated.

After a few weeks, she realized her approach wasn't working. Megan decided to shift her mindset. She started scheduling one-on-ones to rebuild trust, where she asked her team members what they needed from her as a manager. She began focusing on enabling her team rather than controlling them. Slowly but surely, the dynamics improved, and Megan became the respected leader her team needed.

Megan's story is a reminder that leadership is a learning process. Mistakes are inevitable, but they don't define you. How you respond to them does.

Why Leadership is More Than a Promotion

Many people view a management role as the next logical step in their career—a promotion that recognizes their hard work and expertise. But becoming a leader isn't just about climbing the ladder; it's about **stepping into a role of service**.

As a leader, your primary job is no longer to excel individually—it's to help others excel. This mindset shift is critical. Great leaders understand that their success is measured not by their own achievements, but by the success of their team.

Here's what leadership entails:

1. **Responsibility for Others**: Your decisions now impact the careers, morale, and well-being of your team.
2. **A Broader Perspective**: You'll need to think strategically, balancing team needs with organizational goals.
3. **A New Measure of Success**: Your success is now tied to how well your team performs, not just your own output.

Overcoming Self-Doubt: Why You're Ready

It's common to feel imposter syndrome in the early days of management. You might wonder if you're truly qualified to lead, especially if you're managing former peers or more experienced colleagues. Here are some common fears and how to address them:

Fear #1: "I Don't Know Enough About Leadership"

Leadership is not an innate talent; it's a skill that can be learned. No one expects you to have all the answers on Day 1. What matters is your willingness to learn, grow, and adapt.

- **What to do**: Start small. Focus on building trust with your team and mastering the basics of communication and delegation. Leadership development is a journey.

Fear #2: "What if I Make a Mistake?"

You will make mistakes—that's inevitable. Every great leader has stories of early missteps. What sets good managers apart is how they respond to those mistakes.

- **What to do**: Be transparent and accountable. If you misstep, own it, apologize if needed, and focus on how to improve. Your team will respect your humility.

Fear #3: "Will My Team Respect Me?"

Respect is earned, not given. But it's important to remember that you were chosen for this role because others believe in your ability to lead.

- **What to do**: Build credibility through your actions. Show consistency, fairness, and a genuine commitment to your team's success.

Action Steps: Embracing Your New Role

Let's turn theory into practice. Here are three immediate steps to help you embrace your role as a manager:

1. Reflect on Your Leadership "Why"

Take time to define your motivation for becoming a leader. Is it to help others grow? To solve bigger problems? To contribute to your organization in a new way?

> *Reflection Exercise*: Write down your "why" and keep it somewhere visible. Use it

as a guiding principle when faced with tough decisions.

2. Schedule One-on-One Meetings

Your first step as a manager should be to meet with each team member individually. These conversations set the foundation for your relationships.

- **What to ask**:
    - What are your goals?
    - What do you enjoy most about your work?
    - What challenges are you facing?

Tip: Use these meetings to listen more than you speak. Show your team that you value their input and are committed to their success.

3. Set Clear Expectations with Your Boss

Your relationship with your manager will evolve in this new role. Take the initiative to clarify their expectations for you as a leader.

- **Ask questions like**:
    - What are your priorities for our team?
    - How will success be measured in this role?
    - What support can I count on from you?

A Mindset Shift: From Individual to Leader

One of the biggest transitions for new managers is shifting from an "individual contributor" mindset to a "leader" mindset. As an individual contributor, your success was based on your ability to complete tasks. As a leader, your success is based on your ability to **enable others to succeed**.

Here's how the two mindsets differ:

Individual Contributor	Leader
Focus on personal output	Focus on team performance
Measures success by tasks completed	Measures success by team growth
Works independently	Empowers and supports others

This shift isn't easy, but it's essential. Leadership is no longer about what you can do alone—it's about what you can achieve through others.

Closing Thought: Leadership is a Privilege

Becoming a leader is one of the most rewarding challenges you'll ever face. It's an opportunity to shape careers, solve complex problems, and make a lasting impact. But it's also a responsibility—one that requires humility, dedication, and a commitment to growth.

You've earned this role. Now it's time to embrace it, learn from it, and grow into the leader your team deserves.

Chapter 2: Rewiring Relationships: From Peer to Leader

Introduction: A Balancing Act

One of the most challenging parts of becoming a manager is navigating your new relationship with your former peers. Yesterday, you were side-by-side in the trenches, working together as equals. Today, you're their leader. This change can feel awkward, even intimidating—not just for you, but for them too.

You may wonder:

- *"Will my peers still like me?"*
- *"How do I lead without coming across as bossy?"*
- *"What if they resent me for being promoted?"*

These concerns are natural, but here's the good news: While managing former peers is tricky, it's absolutely possible to strike a balance between authority and approachability. The key is to **redefine your relationships intentionally**—with fairness, transparency, and respect.

In this chapter, we'll explore practical strategies for managing this transition with confidence and grace.

The Dynamics of Change

When you're promoted to manage your peers, the dynamics inevitably shift. What once was a horizontal relationship now has a vertical element: You're no longer "one of the gang"—you're the person responsible for making decisions, setting priorities, and holding people accountable.

Here are a few dynamics you're likely to encounter:

1. Friendships Feel Different

Your peers may struggle to adjust to your new role, especially if you were close friends. Conversations that were once casual and open may become guarded. They might wonder whether you'll prioritize the team over personal connections.

- **How to handle it**: Maintain professionalism while still showing you care. Avoid favoritism but don't distance yourself entirely. The goal is to strike a healthy balance between personal connection and professional responsibility.

2. Expectations Change—For Everyone

Your former peers may have expectations about how you'll lead, especially if they're used to collaborating with you as an equal. At the same time, your boss and organization now expect you to deliver results as a manager. Balancing these expectations requires clarity and communication.

- **How to handle it**: Set boundaries and communicate your leadership goals early. Let your team know that your focus is on supporting their success, and be transparent about the changes in your role.

3. Resentment or Jealousy May Arise

Not everyone will be thrilled about your promotion. Some team members may feel overlooked, especially if they were also vying for the role. This can lead to resentment or subtle pushback.

- **How to handle it**: Address resentment proactively by treating everyone fairly and openly. Avoid taking criticism personally, and focus on building trust through consistent actions.

Practical Strategies for Redefining Relationships

1. Have Honest Conversations Early

The sooner you address the shift in dynamics, the better. Schedule one-on-one meetings with each team member to acknowledge the change and share your vision for the team.

- **What to say in one-on-ones**:
  - *"I know this is a transition for both of us. My goal is to make this as smooth as possible."*
  - *"I want to hear your thoughts about what we're doing well and where we can improve."*
  - *"How can I support you as your manager?"*

Tip: Be honest about the fact that this is new for you too. A little vulnerability can go a long way in building trust.

2. Establish Boundaries

Friendships and professional relationships require boundaries, especially now that you're in a leadership role. While you can still be friendly, it's important to avoid situations that could undermine your authority or create perceptions of favoritism.

- **Examples of boundaries to set**:
  - Avoid gossiping or venting about work issues.
  - Be mindful of how personal relationships might impact team dynamics.
  - Treat everyone on the team equally when it comes to work assignments, feedback, and recognition.

3. Focus on Fairness

One of the quickest ways to lose credibility as a leader is to show favoritism. Whether intentional or not, treating some team members differently can create resentment and damage trust.

- **How to stay fair**:
  - Be consistent in how you assign work and provide feedback.

- Use objective criteria when making decisions.
- Regularly seek feedback from your team to ensure everyone feels valued.

4. Earn Respect Through Actions, Not Titles

Just because you've been given the title of manager doesn't mean your team will automatically respect you. Respect must be earned, especially from those who used to see you as a peer.

- **How to build respect**:
    - Lead by example—show the same work ethic and accountability you expect from others.
    - Be decisive but open to input.
    - Acknowledge your mistakes and take responsibility for them.

Common Pitfalls to Avoid

1. Overcompensating to Prove Yourself

Many new managers feel the need to assert their authority early on. This can lead to micromanaging or being overly critical—behaviors that erode trust.

- **What to do instead**: Trust your team to do their jobs. Focus on providing support and removing obstacles rather than controlling every detail.

2. Avoiding Difficult Conversations

It's tempting to sidestep conflicts or uncomfortable topics, especially with former peers. But avoiding these conversations can lead to bigger problems down the road.

- **What to do instead**: Address issues head-on but with empathy. Approach difficult conversations as opportunities for growth, not punishment.

3. Leaning Too Heavily on Friendships

Relying on personal relationships to carry your authority can backfire, especially if your decisions are perceived as biased.

- **What to do instead**: Build credibility through fairness and competence. Let your actions as a leader speak for themselves.

Action Steps: Strengthening Your New Relationships

1. Create a Team Charter

A team charter is a collaborative document that outlines shared goals, values, and expectations. Involving your team in creating this document helps build buy-in and alignment.

- **What to include**:
  - Team goals and priorities.
  - Communication norms (e.g., how meetings are run, response times for emails).
  - Guidelines for collaboration and conflict resolution.

2. Seek Feedback Regularly

Ask your team for feedback on your leadership style and how you can improve. This shows humility and a commitment to growth.

- **Questions to ask**:
    - *"What's one thing I can do better to support you?"*
    - *"Are there any obstacles I can help remove?"*
    - *"How can we improve as a team?"*

3. Invest in Team Building

Strengthening relationships within your team creates a foundation of trust and camaraderie. This is especially important if tensions or jealousy exist.

- **Ideas for team building**:
    - Celebrate wins, both big and small.
    - Host informal check-ins or team lunches to foster connection.
    - Encourage collaboration on key projects.

4. Model Transparency and Accountability

One of the quickest ways to establish trust is to lead by example. Demonstrating transparency in your decisions and accountability for your actions will encourage your team to do the same.

- **What to do**:
    - Be open about why certain decisions are made, especially if they're unpopular.
    - If you make a mistake, own up to it.
    - Acknowledge when you don't have all the answers, and invite collaboration to solve challenges.

5. Be Proactive About Potential Resentment

When managing former peers, unresolved feelings of jealousy, disappointment, or resentment can fester beneath the surface. Addressing these concerns proactively—without being defensive—can help diffuse tension before it grows.

- **What to do**:

- During one-on-ones, ask if there's anything on their mind about the recent changes in the team.
- Reassure them that you value their contributions and that their expertise is critical to the team's success.
- Avoid favoritism or letting personal relationships cloud your decision-making process.

6. Develop Emotional Intelligence (EQ)

Strong emotional intelligence will help you better understand and respond to your team's emotions, making the transition smoother for everyone.

- **What to focus on**:
  - Practice empathy: Try to understand how your team might feel about the transition, especially those who may have also wanted the role.

- Regulate your emotions: Stay calm and composed, especially in tense situations or when facing resistance.
- Build social awareness: Observe the team dynamics and adjust your approach as needed to foster collaboration and harmony.

These six action steps will help you build trust, establish credibility, and set a strong foundation for your new relationships.

Closing Thought: Leadership Through Connection

Stepping into a leadership role is like stepping onto a new stage. The spotlight is on you, and people are watching not just what you say but how you act. When you transition from peer to leader, the stakes feel higher because you're not just managing tasks—you're managing relationships. And relationships, as you know from experience, are complex.

The truth is, leadership is not a one-size-fits-all skill. It's a deeply personal journey. As a new manager, you might feel the temptation to imitate leaders you've admired in the past or lean on authority to establish control. But what your team really wants is authenticity. They don't need you to be the perfect boss; they need you to be a fair, consistent, and approachable leader who genuinely cares about their success.

Think about this: Your peers already know you. They've worked with you, shared jokes with you, and probably even vented with you about work frustrations. That familiarity can be an asset—but only if you handle it thoughtfully. Your goal is not to erase your past relationship with your peers, but to evolve it. You're not leaving the team behind; you're stepping into a role where you serve the team in a different capacity.

As you navigate this shift, focus on building **credibility** and **connection**:

1. **Credibility**: This is earned through your actions, not your title. Show that you're willing to listen,

make tough decisions when necessary, and lead by example. When your team sees that you're fair and consistent, they'll trust you more.
2. **Connection**: Never underestimate the power of personal connection. Great leaders understand that the best results come from relationships built on trust and mutual respect. When your team feels valued as individuals—not just as employees—they'll be more engaged, productive, and motivated.

Remember, you're not alone in this journey. Countless leaders have faced these same challenges and come out stronger. They, too, struggled with awkward transitions, difficult conversations, and moments of doubt. But they succeeded because they made an effort to learn, to grow, and to prioritize their team over their ego.

Here's a mantra to keep in mind as you grow into your leadership role: **"Progress over perfection."** You won't always get it right. There will be days when the conversations feel awkward, the decisions feel too hard, and the path forward feels unclear. That's okay. What matters is that you keep showing up, learning from your mistakes, and striving to lead with integrity and empathy.

Ultimately, leadership is about service. Your role is to create an environment where your team can thrive. When you focus on empowering others, you'll find that the challenges of leadership become opportunities—not just for your team to grow, but for you to grow as well.

So, embrace the discomfort, lean into the learning curve, and trust that you're capable of succeeding in this role. You've earned this opportunity, and with intention and care, you'll grow into a leader your team will respect, trust, and follow.

Chapter 3: Your Leadership Persona: Discovering Your Management Style

Introduction: Becoming the Leader Only You Can Be

Leadership isn't just a skill; it's a personal expression of who you are. Every leader brings their own mix of personality, values, and experiences to the table. Some managers inspire through bold visions and energizing speeches, while others excel by quietly building strong relationships and ensuring steady progress.

The truth is, there's no universal mold for leadership. **The most effective leaders embrace their unique strengths while staying flexible to meet the needs of their team.** Trying to mimic another leader—no matter how effective they are—will come across as inauthentic and unsustainable. Authenticity is key: people follow leaders they trust, and trust is built on genuine actions, not performances.

At the same time, discovering your leadership style doesn't happen overnight. It's a process of self-awareness, trial and error, and learning from others. As you embark on this journey, remember this: your leadership style will evolve. The way you lead on your first day as a manager may look very different a year—or five years—later, as you adapt to new challenges and refine your approach.

This chapter will guide you through the process of uncovering your leadership persona, helping you align your natural tendencies with effective management practices. The goal isn't perfection—it's progress.

The Foundations of Leadership Style

Your leadership style doesn't exist in a vacuum. It's shaped by a variety of influences that define how you think, act, and respond to challenges. Let's break down the four key factors that influence your style:

1. Your Personality

Your personality is the foundation of how you naturally interact with others. Whether you're introverted, extroverted, analytical, or spontaneous, your personality will influence how you lead.

- **Questions to reflect on**:
    - Are you someone who thrives on social interaction, or do you prefer more quiet reflection?
    - Do you enjoy taking quick, decisive action, or do you prefer to analyze and weigh options carefully?

- Do you find satisfaction in tackling tasks directly, or do you feel energized by mentoring and supporting others?

For example, an introverted leader may excel at deep listening and thoughtful problem-solving but need to push themselves to communicate more frequently with their team. An extroverted leader might thrive in inspiring their team but may need to work on giving quieter team members space to contribute.

2. Your Values

Values are the compass that guides your decisions as a leader. They represent what matters most to you in your role and influence how you prioritize, set goals, and interact with your team.

- **Examples of core leadership values**:
    - **Integrity**: Always acting with honesty and fairness, even when it's difficult.
    - **Excellence**: Striving for the highest standards in every task and project.

- **Collaboration**: Encouraging teamwork and building a culture of inclusivity.
- **Empathy**: Valuing the well-being and perspectives of every team member.

Your values will serve as your moral guide when you face tough decisions. For example, if collaboration is a core value, you'll naturally involve your team in brainstorming and problem-solving. If integrity is your guiding principle, you'll prioritize honesty, even if it means owning up to a mistake.

> *Tip*: Identifying your values is a critical step in discovering your leadership style. Take time to reflect on what principles guide your actions both at work and in life.

3. Your Past Experiences

Think about the managers you've worked under. Which ones inspired you? Which ones frustrated you? Whether you realize it or not, these experiences have shaped your ideas about leadership.

- **Reflection exercise**:
    - Recall a manager who had a positive impact on you. What specific behaviors or traits made them effective?
    - Now think about a manager who left a negative impression. What did they do—or fail to do—that hindered the team's success?

These reflections can serve as a blueprint for the kind of leader you want to be—and the kind you want to avoid becoming.

4. Your Team's Needs

No matter how authentic your leadership style is, it also needs to be flexible to meet your team where they are. Every team is different, and their needs should influence how you approach your role.

- **Questions to consider**:

- Are your team members experienced and independent, or do they require more hands-on guidance?
- Are they comfortable with ambiguity, or do they thrive with clear instructions and structure?
- What motivates them—financial incentives, growth opportunities, recognition, or something else?

For example, a team of seasoned professionals might thrive with an autonomous leadership style, while a group of new hires may need more coaching and regular feedback.

The Importance of Authenticity

Authenticity is one of the most important traits a leader can have. Why? Because leadership is built on trust, and trust is built on honesty. Your team doesn't need you to have all the answers, but they do need you to be genuine in your actions, words, and intentions.

The Risks of Inauthenticity

When leaders try to adopt a style that doesn't align with who they truly are, it often backfires:

- **Erosion of trust**: If your actions feel forced or inconsistent, your team may question your motives.
- **Strained relationships**: People are drawn to leaders who are relatable. Pretending to be someone you're not creates distance.
- **Burnout**: It's exhausting to maintain a persona that doesn't reflect your true self.

   Example: If you're naturally a reserved person, trying to be a high-energy cheerleader may come across as insincere. Instead, lean into your strengths as a thoughtful and composed leader, while finding ways to inspire and motivate in a way that feels authentic to you.

While every leader is unique, most leadership styles fall into broad categories. Understanding these styles can help you identify where your natural tendencies lie and how you can adapt as needed. Below are eight widely recognized leadership styles, including their strengths, challenges, and the scenarios where they work best:

1. The Visionary Leader

- **Strengths**: Sets a bold direction, inspires innovation, and motivates the team with a clear long-term goal.
- **Challenges**: Can overlook day-to-day execution or neglect team input in pursuit of the vision.
- **Best for**: Teams that thrive on creativity and big-picture thinking, especially in dynamic industries like tech, startups, or design.

Example: Steve Jobs (Apple) was a quintessential visionary leader. His ability to articulate a clear vision—like creating devices that "put a dent in the universe"—

inspired his team to develop groundbreaking innovations.

2. The Democratic Leader

- **Strengths**: Encourages collaboration, values team input, and fosters strong relationships.
- **Challenges**: May struggle to make quick or unilateral decisions in high-pressure situations.
- **Best for**: Teams that value inclusivity, creativity, and shared decision-making, such as those in non-profits or creative agencies.

Example: Satya Nadella (Microsoft) transformed the company's culture by fostering collaboration and open dialogue, encouraging employees to contribute to the company's innovation strategy.

3. The Coaching Leader

- **Strengths**: Focuses on individual growth, helping team members develop their skills and careers.

- **Challenges**: Can lose sight of team goals by spending too much time on one-on-one coaching.
- **Best for**: Teams eager to learn and grow, such as junior employees or those looking to advance their careers.

Example: Leaders in mentorship-driven organizations, like Sheryl Sandberg (Meta), often employ a coaching approach, guiding employees toward personal and professional growth.

4. The Directive Leader

- **Strengths**: Provides structure and clarity, especially during crises or when tackling complex projects.
- **Challenges**: May come across as overly controlling or rigid if not balanced with empathy.
- **Best for**: Teams that need strong guidance, such as in high-pressure industries like healthcare, manufacturing, or the military.

Example: General Dwight D. Eisenhower during World War II demonstrated directive leadership by maintaining clear priorities and giving decisive orders in high-stakes scenarios.

5. The Servant Leader

- **Strengths**: Prioritizes the well-being and needs of the team, fostering loyalty and trust.
- **Challenges**: Can risk neglecting broader organizational goals to focus on individual team members.
- **Best for**: Building team morale and trust over the long term, especially in fields like education, social services, or customer service.

Example: Howard Schultz (Starbucks) is often cited as a servant leader, emphasizing employee well-being through benefits like healthcare and tuition reimbursement.

6. The Transformational Leader

- **Strengths**: Focuses on inspiring change, driving innovation, and challenging the status quo.
- **Challenges**: May struggle with the practical implementation of ideas, requiring strong execution-focused support.
- **Best for**: Teams in fast-changing industries or organizations that need reinvention, like startups or companies undergoing a digital transformation.

Example: Jeff Bezos (Amazon) is a transformational leader, constantly pushing his teams to innovate, experiment, and disrupt traditional markets. His leadership transformed Amazon from an online bookstore into a global powerhouse.

7. The Transactional Leader

- **Strengths**: Emphasizes structure, rewards, and penalties to drive performance, ensuring accountability and clear expectations.

- **Challenges**: May stifle creativity or fail to motivate employees intrinsically, as the focus is heavily on extrinsic rewards.
- **Best for**: Teams in highly regulated or repetitive industries, such as finance, operations, or logistics, where consistency and compliance are critical.

Example: A call center manager who uses metrics like call times and customer satisfaction scores, rewarding top performers with bonuses, exemplifies transactional leadership.

8. The Laissez-Faire Leader

- **Strengths**: Provides high levels of autonomy, trusting team members to self-manage and make decisions.
- **Challenges**: Can lead to a lack of direction or accountability if team members don't have the necessary experience or motivation.

- **Best for**: Highly skilled and independent teams, such as research scientists, software developers, or creative professionals.

Example: Warren Buffett (Berkshire Hathaway) adopts a laissez-faire leadership style, giving the CEOs of his subsidiary companies freedom to run their businesses while providing guidance when necessary.

Each leadership style has its strengths and limitations, and no single approach works for every situation. The most effective leaders are those who can adapt their style to the context, their team's needs, and the challenges at hand.

As you discover your own leadership persona, reflect on these styles. Which one feels most natural to you? Which one challenges you to grow? By blending authenticity with flexibility, you'll find a style that aligns with your strengths and empowers your team to thrive.

Reflection Exercise: Which Style Fits You?

Think about the leadership style descriptions above. Which one resonates most with your natural tendencies? Which one feels least comfortable? Understanding your baseline tendencies will help you identify areas where you excel and where you may need to stretch.

Action Steps: Building Your Leadership Persona

1. **Take a Leadership Assessment**: Tools like DISC, Gallup StrengthsFinder, or MBTI can offer valuable insights into your leadership tendencies.
2. **Experiment and Reflect**: Try applying different styles to different scenarios and evaluate the results.
3. **Ask for Feedback**: Your team's perspective can reveal blind spots in your leadership approach.
4. **Develop a Leadership Philosophy**: Write a short statement that summarizes what kind of leader you aspire to be, including your core values and priorities.

Closing Thought: Leadership is a Journey of Self-Discovery

Becoming a leader isn't about copying others or pretending to be someone you're not. It's about growing into the best version of yourself. Your leadership style will evolve as you gain experience, face challenges, and learn from your successes and failures.

The key is to stay true to your values, embrace your strengths, and remain open to growth. Authenticity, combined with a willingness to adapt, will make you the kind of leader your team trusts, respects, and follows with confidence.

Chapter 4: Adopting a Leader's Mindset

Introduction: Thinking Like a Leader

You've stepped into a new role, one that comes with greater responsibility, influence, and complexity. As a leader, the way you think about your work—and your team's work—needs to fundamentally change. You're no longer the star player on the field; you're the coach, orchestrating the plays, analyzing the game, and making decisions that enable your team to win.

The skills that made you successful as an individual contributor—your ability to execute tasks, solve problems independently, and focus on your own performance—won't be enough in this new role. Leadership demands a new mindset: one that prioritizes the team over the individual, strategy over tactics, and foresight over reaction.

Many first-time managers find this shift daunting because it requires letting go of the things they were good at. It's tempting to step back into familiar territory—to take on tasks yourself or micromanage team members to ensure everything is done "right." But great leadership is about trusting and enabling others to succeed, even when it feels uncomfortable at first.

Adopting a leader's mindset means seeing your role through a new lens:

- **You're not just doing the work anymore; you're guiding others to do it well.**
- **You're not just solving problems; you're anticipating them and creating systems to avoid them.**
- **You're not focused solely on today; you're thinking about how today's decisions impact the future.**

In this chapter, we'll explore the key mindset shifts every new manager needs to make to thrive in their role. We'll also provide practical strategies to help you transition from thinking like a contributor to thinking like a leader.

Key Mindset Shifts for New Leaders

1. From "Doing" to "Enabling"

One of the most significant challenges for new managers is letting go of the work they used to do themselves. As an individual contributor, your value came from your ability to complete tasks efficiently and effectively. Now, as a leader, your value comes from your ability to empower others to complete those tasks.

- **What it means**:
    - Your primary role is no longer to do the work, but to create the conditions for your team to succeed. This includes delegating

tasks, providing resources, and offering guidance when needed.
- Leadership isn't about being the smartest person in the room—it's about bringing out the best in the people around you.
- **Why this is hard**:
  - You may feel tempted to take on tasks yourself because you're confident in your abilities and want to ensure things are done "right."
  - Letting go of control can feel risky, especially if you're accountable for your team's performance.

Example: Imagine you're a former sales rep who's now managing a sales team. In your previous role, you thrived on closing deals. But as a manager, your time is better spent coaching team members on how to close deals themselves, rather than stepping in to do it for them.

- **Tips to succeed**:
  - Start small: Delegate a task or project to a trusted team member and resist the urge to micromanage.
  - Shift your perspective: View delegation not as giving up control, but as an opportunity to develop your team's skills.

2. From Short-Term Focus to Long-Term Thinking

As a contributor, your primary focus was often on completing tasks and meeting immediate deadlines. Leaders, however, need to think beyond the day-to-day. Your job is to align your team's work with long-term goals and anticipate future challenges or opportunities.

- **What it means**:
  - Balancing immediate needs with strategic priorities. You still need to hit short-term targets, but you must also think about how today's work sets the stage for future success.

- Being proactive rather than reactive. Instead of just solving problems as they arise, you'll need to identify potential risks and plan for them in advance.
- **Why this is hard**:
  - It's easy to get caught up in urgent tasks and neglect long-term planning.
  - Strategic thinking requires stepping back and looking at the bigger picture, which can feel uncomfortable if you're used to being "in the weeds."

Example: If your team is working on a product launch, it's not just about meeting the launch date. It's also about considering how the product fits into the company's long-term strategy and ensuring your team is prepared for post-launch support.

- **Tips to succeed**:
  - Schedule dedicated time each week to focus on long-term planning.

- Communicate the "why" behind your team's work to help them understand how their efforts contribute to larger goals.

3. From "Me" to "We"

Leadership is a team sport. While your individual performance mattered most in your previous role, your success as a leader is now measured by your team's success. This requires shifting your focus from individual achievements to collective outcomes.

- **What it means**:
    - Creating a culture of collaboration, where team members feel empowered to contribute and support one another.
    - Taking responsibility for your team's failures as well as their successes. Great leaders own their team's challenges rather than placing blame.
- **Why this is hard**:
    - It can be tempting to focus on your own performance metrics, especially if you're

used to being recognized for your individual contributions.
- Balancing the needs of the group with the needs of individuals can be tricky.

Example: When a project succeeds, shift the focus from "I led this effort" to "Our team worked together to make this happen." Publicly celebrate your team's contributions while privately reflecting on your role in their success.

- **Tips to succeed**:
  - Regularly ask yourself, "What does my team need from me to succeed?"
  - Build trust by showing empathy and understanding individual team members' strengths and challenges.

4. From Reacting to Anticipating

As a contributor, much of your work was reactive: responding to emails, solving problems as they arose, and hitting deadlines. Leaders, however, need to take a proactive approach, anticipating challenges before they occur and planning for the future.

- **What it means**:
    - Paying attention to patterns or recurring issues and addressing the root causes.
    - Thinking ahead about resources, timelines, and potential obstacles.
- **Why this is hard**:
    - It's easy to fall into a cycle of constantly "putting out fires" rather than addressing systemic issues.
    - Developing the habit of proactive thinking takes time and practice.

Example: If your team regularly struggles to meet deadlines, don't just push them to work harder. Instead, analyze the root cause—Are deadlines unrealistic? Are resources inadequate? Then implement changes to prevent the issue from recurring.

- **Tips to succeed**:
  - Schedule regular "review and plan" sessions to identify potential challenges.
  - Encourage your team to share insights and flag issues early.

Practical Strategies for Adopting a Leader's Mindset

1. Set Clear Priorities

Leadership requires juggling competing demands, so it's critical to identify and focus on what matters most.

- **How to set priorities**:
  - Use tools like the Eisenhower Matrix (urgent vs. important) to organize tasks.
  - Regularly communicate priorities to your team to ensure alignment.

2. Focus on Communication

Clear communication is the foundation of effective leadership. Your team relies on you to set expectations, provide guidance, and share updates on progress and goals.

- **Tips for success**:
  - Practice active listening during one-on-ones.
  - Be transparent about decisions, especially those that impact the team.

3. Build a Support Network

Leadership can feel isolating, especially when you're navigating new challenges. Surround yourself with mentors, peers, and resources to help you grow.

- **How to build support**:
  - Seek out other managers for advice and perspective.
  - Find a mentor within or outside your organization.

4. Develop Self-Awareness

Great leaders know their strengths, weaknesses, and blind spots.

- **How to improve self-awareness**:
    - Reflect regularly on your leadership actions and decisions.
    - Ask for feedback from your team and act on it.

Closing Thought: Leadership is a New Way of Seeing

Adopting a leader's mindset is not an overnight process—it's a journey of growth, self-reflection, and learning. This role challenges you to think differently, prioritize differently, and see your work through the lens of empowerment rather than execution.

Remember, leadership isn't about being the best at everything—it's about creating the best environment for your team to thrive. By focusing on enabling others, thinking long-term, fostering collaboration, and anticipating challenges, you'll not only grow as a leader but also build a team that succeeds because of your influence.

Leadership is less about doing and more about **becoming**. It's a transformation that requires patience, intentionality, and a willingness to adapt. Embrace this new way of seeing the world, and you'll find that the rewards of leadership—helping others succeed, solving complex challenges, and driving meaningful impact—are worth every step of the journey.

Chapter 5: Communication is Key: Leading Through Words

Introduction: The Power of Communication

Imagine you're in a meeting with your team. You've just outlined a new project that needs to be completed in record time. You think you've explained it clearly, but the moment the meeting ends, the questions start pouring in:

- *"What's the priority—quality or speed?"*
- *"Who's in charge of the timeline?"*
- *"What exactly are we supposed to deliver?"*

Suddenly, the project feels chaotic, not because your team isn't capable, but because the expectations weren't communicated clearly.

This scenario illustrates a hard truth: as a leader, communication can make or break your success.

Great communication isn't just about delivering information—it's about ensuring that information is understood and acted upon. Leaders must go beyond words to connect with their teams, inspire action, and foster alignment.

But communication doesn't stop with speaking; it's equally about listening. Your team's feedback, concerns, and ideas are invaluable. By creating a culture of open dialogue, you'll build trust, uncover blind spots, and empower your team to thrive.

In this chapter, we'll explore how to communicate effectively in key leadership situations, provide actionable strategies for improvement, and help you master the art of leading through words.

The Core Principles of Effective Communication (Expanded)

1. Clarity is Everything

Effective leaders eliminate ambiguity. Without clear communication, misunderstandings arise, mistakes happen, and productivity suffers.

- **Practical Strategies for Clarity:**
    - Repeat key points: People rarely absorb everything the first time. Reinforce important messages during meetings and follow up in writing.
    - Chunk your information: Break complex instructions into smaller, more digestible parts.
    - Ask for confirmation: After explaining something, ask your team to summarize their understanding. This prevents misalignment.

Scenario: You assign a task to your team with a vague deadline of "next week." To ensure clarity, instead say, "Please submit the draft by 3 p.m. on Wednesday, so I can review it by Thursday morning."

Case Study 1: The Clarity Challenge

Scenario:
Maria is a first-time manager leading a team of four marketing specialists. She assigns a project to "develop a social media strategy for the new product launch." Maria assumes the team understands what she means, but as the deadline approaches, she realizes everyone interpreted the task differently. One team member focused on creating a content calendar, while another worked on paid ad campaigns. The result? A disjointed presentation with missing key components.

Analysis:
Maria's lack of clarity caused the team to waste time and miss expectations. She realized that by providing

specific instructions, she could have prevented the confusion.

Solution:

Maria learned to clarify tasks by:

1. **Defining the deliverable**: "Create a comprehensive strategy document outlining target audiences, content themes, platforms, and budgets."
2. **Setting roles**: Assigning individual responsibilities, like one person for content, another for analytics, etc.
3. **Establishing checkpoints**: Scheduling a mid-project review to ensure alignment.

Key Lesson:

Ambiguity leads to misalignment. Clear instructions, role assignments, and milestones ensure everyone is on the same page.

2. Tailor Your Message to Your Audience

Your team is made up of individuals with diverse personalities, work styles, and preferences. Communicating effectively means understanding these differences and adapting your approach accordingly.

- **Deep Dive into Tailoring:**
    - The Detail-Oriented: These team members want facts, data, and specifics. Provide them with thorough explanations and supporting documents.
    - The Big-Picture Thinkers: Focus on overarching goals and avoid overwhelming them with too many details.
    - The Introverts: They may process information internally and need time to reflect. Give them space before expecting input.
    - The Extroverts: These individuals thrive in dynamic conversations. Engage them in brainstorming and discussions.

Example: When presenting a new project plan, you might use a data-heavy slide deck for your analytical thinkers and follow it up with a one-on-one conversation for team members who process better in smaller settings.

Case Study 2: Tailoring Communication to the Audience

Scenario:

John manages a cross-functional team working on a software rollout. During a weekly meeting, he gives a detailed 20-minute technical explanation of the system's backend features. The developers are engaged, but the sales and marketing team members tune out, frustrated by the technical jargon. Later, one marketing lead privately complains, "I didn't understand half of what was said, and I still don't know how this impacts my work."

Analysis:

John failed to tailor his message to his audience. While the technical details were relevant for the developers, the sales and marketing team needed a high-level overview focused on how the software would affect their work.

Solution:

John began segmenting his communication:

1. For technical staff, he shared detailed specs and hosted Q&A sessions.
2. For non-technical roles, he created a summary slide deck highlighting user benefits, timelines, and team-specific impacts.
3. He encouraged team members to ask clarifying questions during meetings to avoid miscommunication.

Key Lesson:

Different audiences require different levels of detail. Understanding your team's varying needs ensures that your message resonates with everyone.

3. Listen More Than You Speak

Great leaders understand that listening is more than just hearing words—it's about understanding the deeper message behind them.

- **How to Practice Active Listening:**
    - Be fully present: Eliminate distractions during conversations—put your phone away and maintain eye contact.
    - Use verbal cues: Say things like, "I understand," or "That makes sense," to show engagement.
    - Ask clarifying questions: If someone says they're "struggling with workload," ask, "Can you tell me more about what's making it difficult?"
    - Follow up: If a team member shares a concern, circle back later to check if it's been resolved.

    Example: During a one-on-one, a team member mentions feeling undervalued.

Instead of brushing it off, respond with, "I hear you. Can you share what would make you feel more appreciated?" This opens the door for a productive conversation.

Case Study 3: The Listening Leader

Scenario:

Priya notices that one of her team members, Tom, has become less engaged during meetings and isn't meeting his usual performance standards. Instead of jumping to conclusions, Priya schedules a one-on-one conversation and practices active listening.

During the meeting, Priya asks, "I've noticed you've seemed a bit distracted lately. Is there something on your mind?" Initially hesitant, Tom eventually opens up, sharing that he's overwhelmed by personal issues and is struggling to manage his workload.

Analysis:

By creating a safe space and truly listening, Priya uncovers the root cause of Tom's performance issues.

Had she ignored the signs or dismissed his struggles, the problem could have escalated, potentially leading to burnout or even turnover.

Solution:

Priya takes action by:

1. Adjusting Tom's workload temporarily to give him breathing room.
2. Offering resources like the company's Employee Assistance Program (EAP).
3. Scheduling a follow-up to check in on his progress.

Key Lesson:

Active listening builds trust and helps uncover underlying issues that affect performance. Leaders who listen with empathy can address problems proactively and support their team's well-being.

4. Consistency Builds Trust

Inconsistency erodes trust faster than almost anything else. Your team needs to know what to expect from you—not just in how you communicate, but in how you act.

- **Deep Dive into Consistency:**
    - Deliver on promises: If you say you'll follow up by Friday, make sure you do. Inconsistencies create doubt about your reliability.
    - Enforce rules equally: Don't play favorites. Treat everyone on your team with the same level of accountability.
    - Be emotionally consistent: Avoid mood swings that leave your team guessing whether you'll be approachable or irritable.

Scenario: If you establish a policy of turning off cameras during virtual meetings to minimize Zoom fatigue, ensure you follow the rule yourself. If you suddenly keep yours on, your team may feel pressured to do the same.

Mastering Key Leadership Conversations

1. Motivating Your Team

Motivating your team isn't about cheerleading or empty platitudes. It's about connecting their work to a meaningful purpose.

- **How to Inspire Through Communication:**
    - Use storytelling: Share how their work impacts customers, the organization, or the team.
    - Personalize motivation: Learn what drives each team member. Some are motivated by recognition, others by growth opportunities.
    - Highlight progress: Regularly remind your team of what they've accomplished and what's ahead.

    Example: Instead of saying, "We need to meet this deadline," say, "Completing this project on time will help us land a critical client and secure funding for the next phase of development."

2. Giving Constructive Feedback

Feedback is one of the most valuable tools in a leader's toolkit, but it's also one of the hardest to deliver well.

- **The Feedback Formula:**
    - Start with the positive: Highlight what's working before addressing areas for improvement.
    - Be behavior-focused: Avoid saying, "You're not a good team player." Instead, say, "In our last meeting, I noticed you interrupted others several times. Let's work on ensuring everyone has a chance to share."
    - Collaborate on solutions: Ask the team member what they think could help resolve the issue.

3. Resolving Conflicts

Conflict resolution requires empathy, fairness, and a solutions-focused approach.

- **How to Manage Conflict:**
    - Separate the person from the problem: Address the issue without attacking the individual.
    - Encourage dialogue: Allow each party to share their perspective without interruptions.
    - Focus on the outcome: Shift the conversation from "who's right" to "how can we move forward."

Example: Two team members argue over resource allocation. Instead of taking sides, guide the discussion by saying, "Our shared goal is to complete the project on time. Let's work together to determine the best way to distribute resources."

Case Study 5: Resolving Team Conflict

Scenario:

A heated argument breaks out during a meeting between two team members, Alex and Jordan. Alex accuses Jordan of not pulling their weight, while Jordan counters that Alex has been micromanaging and creating unnecessary delays. The rest of the team grows uncomfortable, and the meeting ends without resolving the tension.

Analysis:

Unresolved conflicts like this can damage team morale and productivity. As the leader, it's Priya's responsibility to address the issue and mediate a resolution.

Solution:

Priya takes the following steps:

1. **Hold private conversations**: She meets with Alex and Jordan individually to hear their perspectives without interruptions.
2. **Facilitate a joint meeting**: She brings them together and sets ground rules for respectful communication. Priya asks each person to share

their concerns and then guides the discussion toward finding common ground.
3. **Focus on the team's goals**: Priya reframes the conflict as a shared problem, saying, "Our goal is to complete this project successfully. Let's figure out how we can work together to make that happen."
4. **Establish next steps**: Priya creates an action plan that clarifies roles and responsibilities for both team members moving forward.

Key Lesson:
Conflict is inevitable, but effective leaders address it head-on, creating a safe environment for dialogue and fostering collaboration.

4. Communicating Difficult Decisions

Delivering tough news—like a budget cut or a missed target—requires a mix of transparency and empathy.

- **How to Communicate Clearly:**

- Be honest: Share the decision and the rationale behind it, even if it's unpopular.
- Show empathy: Acknowledge the impact the decision may have on your team.
- Provide a path forward: End the conversation by focusing on next steps or solutions.

Example: Instead of saying, "The company has decided to cut bonuses," say, "Due to budget constraints, bonuses won't be issued this year. I know this is disappointing. Let's discuss other ways we can recognize your hard work."

Case Study 4: Delivering Tough News with Transparency

Scenario:

Sarah's company has decided to freeze annual bonuses due to economic challenges. As a team leader, it falls on Sarah to deliver this news to her team of 12 employees.

She knows the decision will upset them, as many rely on bonuses to supplement their income.

Analysis:

Sarah recognizes that how she communicates this message will impact team morale. If she's vague or dismissive, her team might feel undervalued. If she's honest but empathetic, they're more likely to understand the context behind the decision.

Solution:

Sarah prepares by:

1. **Gathering the facts**: She ensures she understands the company's reasoning, the financial outlook, and what steps are being taken to support employees in other ways.
2. **Framing the conversation**: She acknowledges the impact of the decision and shows empathy.
3. **Offering a path forward**: She highlights other opportunities for recognition, like spot bonuses or public acknowledgment of achievements.

During the meeting, Sarah says:

"I know this decision is disappointing, and I want to acknowledge how hard everyone has worked this year. The bonus freeze is due to the economic challenges we're facing, but I want to reassure you that leadership is focused on protecting jobs and ensuring stability for the company. Let's work together to find other ways to recognize and reward the amazing work you've done."

Key Lesson:
Delivering bad news requires transparency, empathy, and a focus on the next steps. Clear, honest communication helps maintain trust during difficult times.

Practical Strategies for Improving Communication

1. Hold Effective Meetings

- **Deep Dive:**
    - Start every meeting with a clear purpose. For example, "This meeting is to finalize the Q1 sales strategy."

- Assign roles: Note-taker, facilitator, and presenter roles can keep meetings efficient.

2. Use Visual Aids

A picture is worth a thousand words. Tools like slides, diagrams, or dashboards can make complex ideas more accessible.

3. Ask Open-Ended Questions

- **Examples:**
    - *"What's one thing you'd change about our workflow?"*
    - *"How can we improve communication as a team?"*

4. Practice Transparency

When you're open about both successes and challenges, your team feels included and respected.

Closing Thought: Leadership Through Communication

Communication isn't just a skill—it's the lifeblood of leadership. As a manager, the words you choose and the way you deliver them shape your team's understanding, trust, and morale. Whether you're motivating your team, delivering feedback, or resolving conflicts, remember that your goal is always to create clarity, foster connection, and inspire action.

But great communication doesn't happen by accident—it's something you practice, refine, and adapt over time. By committing to improve every interaction, you'll not only grow as a leader but also build a culture where people feel valued, understood, and empowered to contribute their best.

Chapter 6: Delegation 101: Letting Go Without Losing Control

Introduction: The Art of Delegation

One of the biggest transitions for new managers is the shift from *doing* to *leading*. As an individual contributor, your value was measured by how much you personally accomplished. But as a manager, your value comes from how well your team performs. This means learning to delegate—assigning tasks and responsibilities to your team members so you can focus on higher-level priorities.

For many first-time managers, delegation is uncomfortable. You might feel like you're burdening your team, or worry they won't do the work as well as you could. Maybe you've even thought, *"It's faster if I just do it myself."*

But here's the truth: failing to delegate effectively limits both your growth as a leader and your team's growth as contributors. When you try to do everything yourself, you risk burnout and rob your team members of the opportunity to develop their skills and take ownership of their work.

Delegation isn't about dumping tasks on others—it's about empowering your team while creating space for you to focus on the bigger picture. Done right, it builds trust, accountability, and stronger results for everyone.

In this chapter, we'll explore the mindset shift required for delegation, the practical steps to delegate effectively, and strategies to overcome common challenges.

Why Delegation is Hard for New Managers

1. Perfectionism

You might believe no one else can do the job as well as you can. This leads to micromanaging or avoiding delegation altogether.

- *Mindset shift*: Delegation isn't about perfection; it's about progress. Even if the result isn't exactly how you'd do it, it's an opportunity for your team to learn and improve.

2. Fear of Losing Control

Letting go of tasks can feel risky, especially if you're ultimately responsible for the outcome.

- *Mindset shift*: Delegation doesn't mean abandoning responsibility. You're still guiding and supporting your team—you're just empowering them to execute.

3. Misconceptions About Burdening Your Team

You might feel guilty assigning more work to your team, especially if they're already busy.

- *Mindset shift*: Delegation is an investment in your team's growth. By giving them new responsibilities, you're helping them build skills and confidence.

The Benefits of Delegation

Delegation isn't just about making your workload more manageable—it benefits your entire team.

- **For you**:
    - Frees up your time for strategic thinking and leadership responsibilities.
    - Reduces stress and prevents burnout.
- **For your team**:
    - Builds trust and confidence by showing you believe in their abilities.
    - Provides opportunities for growth and skill development.
- **For the organization**:
    - Increases efficiency by ensuring tasks are handled by the right people.
    - Encourages collaboration and accountability across the team.

How to Delegate Effectively

1. Choose the Right Tasks to Delegate

Not all tasks are suitable for delegation. Focus on the tasks that:

- Can be done by someone else without requiring your specific expertise.
- Provide growth opportunities for your team members.
- Free up your time for higher-priority responsibilities.

Example: If you're preparing a detailed report, delegate the data collection and initial analysis to a team member while you focus on synthesizing the key insights.

2. Match the Task to the Right Person

Delegating isn't just about offloading work—it's about aligning the task with the skills, interests, and development goals of your team members.

- **Consider**:
    - Who has the skills to handle the task?
    - Who would benefit from the challenge?

- Who has the bandwidth to take on additional responsibilities?

Example: If a team member is looking to develop leadership skills, assign them a project that involves managing others or coordinating across departments.

3. Set Clear Expectations

Ambiguity is the enemy of effective delegation. Ensure your team member understands:

- **The outcome**: What does success look like?
- **The timeline**: When is the task or project due?
- **The resources**: What tools or support do they need?

Example: Instead of saying, "Can you handle the presentation?" say, "Please prepare a 10-minute presentation on the marketing campaign results by Tuesday at 3 p.m. I'd like it to include key metrics, trends, and next steps."

4. Provide the Right Level of Support

Delegation doesn't mean disappearing—it means being available to guide without micromanaging.

- **How to balance support**:
    - Check in periodically to answer questions or address challenges.
    - Resist the urge to take over or redo their work unless absolutely necessary.

    Example: After delegating a task, say, "Let me know if you run into any roadblocks. I'll check in on Thursday to see how things are progressing."

5. Give Feedback and Recognition

Once the task is complete, provide constructive feedback on what went well and where there's room for improvement. Recognize their contributions to build confidence and trust.

Example: "Great job on the report! The data analysis was thorough, and your visuals were clear and engaging. For next time, let's focus on making the executive summary more concise."

Exercise 1: Identify Tasks You Can Delegate

Purpose: To help you analyze your workload and determine which tasks are suitable for delegation.

1. **Make a Task List**: Write down all your current responsibilities. Include recurring tasks, one-time projects, and administrative duties.
2. **Categorize Tasks**: Divide your list into three categories:
    - **Tasks Only You Can Do**: These are high-level strategic tasks or responsibilities tied directly to your role.
    - **Tasks You Can Delegate**: These are tasks that don't require your unique expertise and can be handled by others.

- **Tasks to Eliminate**: Are there low-value tasks that don't add much to your team's or organization's success? Consider whether they can be stopped altogether.
3. **Prioritize Delegation**: From the "Tasks You Can Delegate" list, choose 1–2 tasks to delegate this week.

Reflection: After completing the exercise, ask yourself:

- How much time will I save by delegating these tasks?
- Who on my team would benefit from handling these responsibilities?

Overcoming Delegation Challenges

Challenge 1: "They Might Fail"

Fear of mistakes often holds managers back from delegating. But failure is a natural part of growth.

- **Solution**: Frame mistakes as learning opportunities. If a team member struggles with a task, guide them through the solution and discuss how they can improve next time.

  Example: If a team member misses a deadline, ask, "What happened? How can we adjust the process to ensure deadlines are met in the future?"

Challenge 2: "It's Faster If I Do It Myself"

While it may seem quicker to handle tasks yourself, this approach creates long-term inefficiencies by making you a bottleneck.

- **Solution**: Think of delegation as an upfront investment. It may take time to train someone, but once they're equipped to handle the task, you'll free up your bandwidth permanently.

  Example: If you delegate creating reports to someone else, you might spend an hour training them initially, but you'll save hours of work every week moving forward.

Challenge 3: Micromanaging

Hovering over your team after delegating a task undermines trust and defeats the purpose of delegation.

- **Solution**: Set clear expectations upfront and trust your team to deliver. Focus on outcomes rather than the exact process they use.

    Example: Instead of checking on progress every day, set milestones for review (e.g., "Let's touch base at the halfway point to ensure everything's on track").

Practical Strategies for Delegation

1. Start Small

If you're new to delegation, start with low-risk tasks and gradually build up to more complex responsibilities.

2. Use a Delegation Checklist

Before delegating, ask yourself:

- What's the objective of the task?
- Who is the best fit for this task?
- What resources or information will they need?
- How will I measure success?

3. Create a Feedback Loop

After delegating, schedule time to review the results and discuss lessons learned. This ensures continuous improvement for both you and your team.

Closing Thought: Empowerment Through Delegation

Delegation is more than a management tool—it's an act of trust and empowerment. By delegating effectively, you're not just lightening your own workload; you're investing in your team's growth, building their confidence, and creating a culture of collaboration and accountability.

Yes, it can feel uncomfortable at first. Letting go of tasks you once excelled at and trusting others to deliver can be a leap of faith. But the rewards far outweigh the risks. Delegation frees you to focus on the bigger picture, develops the skills of your team, and ultimately leads to better results for everyone.

Remember, great leaders don't try to do it all themselves. They build strong, capable teams by empowering others to step up and shine.

"Delegation isn't just a skill—it's a mindset shift. As you work through these exercises, remember that the goal isn't just to lighten your workload—it's to empower your team and create a culture of trust and accountability. Start small, reflect on your progress, and keep challenging yourself to let go and lead."

Chapter 7: The Feedback Formula: Giving and Receiving Input

Introduction: Feedback as a Leadership Superpower

Feedback is the lifeblood of leadership. It's how you guide your team, align performance with goals, and foster continuous growth. Done well, feedback can boost morale, strengthen relationships, and improve results. But done poorly—or not at all—it can lead to confusion, resentment, and stagnation.

For many managers, giving feedback is one of the most uncomfortable aspects of leadership. You might worry about upsetting your team, damaging relationships, or coming across as overly critical. Similarly, receiving feedback from your team can feel intimidating, as it exposes blind spots or areas where you might need to improve.

The good news? Feedback is a skill you can develop, and when approached with intention and care, it becomes one of the most powerful tools in your leadership toolkit. In this chapter, you'll learn how to deliver feedback that inspires improvement, receive input with an open mind, and create a culture where feedback flows freely in both directions.

The Two Sides of Feedback

1. Giving Feedback

When you think of feedback, you might immediately picture a formal performance review. But effective feedback is an ongoing process, not a once-a-year event. It's the small, timely conversations that have the greatest impact.

Feedback can take two forms:

- **Positive Feedback**: Recognizing achievements, reinforcing good behavior, and boosting confidence.

- **Constructive Feedback**: Identifying areas for improvement, offering guidance, and encouraging growth.

2. Receiving Feedback

Leadership isn't just about giving feedback—it's about being open to receiving it as well. Your team's insights can help you grow, improve your leadership style, and build trust. When you actively seek and act on feedback, you demonstrate humility and a commitment to self-improvement.

The Feedback Formula: How to Give Feedback Effectively

Giving effective feedback requires a structured approach that focuses on clarity, respect, and actionable insights. Use the following framework to guide your conversations:

1. Be Timely

Feedback is most impactful when delivered as close to the event as possible. Waiting weeks or months reduces its relevance and makes it harder for the recipient to act on.

> *Example*: If a team member delivers an exceptional presentation, don't wait until the next review cycle to recognize their effort. Tell them immediately after the meeting: "Your presentation was clear and persuasive, especially how you outlined the client's ROI."

2. Be Specific

Avoid vague statements like "Good job" or "You need to improve." Instead, focus on specific behaviors or outcomes. This makes feedback more actionable.

> *Example*: Instead of saying, "Your report wasn't great," say, "The report was missing key data in the financial section. Next time,

let's ensure all financial metrics are included to give a complete picture."

3. Focus on Behavior, Not Personality

Feedback should address actions, not character traits. Critiquing someone's personality feels personal and can create defensiveness.

> *Example*: Say, "In today's meeting, you interrupted several colleagues before they finished speaking," rather than, "You're always interrupting people."

4. Provide a Path Forward

Feedback without solutions can feel discouraging. Always pair constructive criticism with actionable suggestions for improvement.

> *Example*: If a team member struggles with time management, say, "I noticed some delays in your recent project. Let's set up a

weekly check-in to help prioritize tasks and track progress."

5. Balance Positive and Constructive Feedback

Feedback should reinforce what's working, not just highlight what's not. Use the **"feedback sandwich"** technique:

1. Start with positive feedback.
2. Address the area for improvement.
3. End with encouragement or another positive comment.

Example: "Your analysis of the market trends was excellent—really thorough and insightful. One thing to work on is simplifying your visuals for the presentation so they're easier to follow. Overall, great job pulling all the data together so efficiently!"

How to Receive Feedback Like a Pro

Receiving feedback can be uncomfortable, especially if it's critical. But leaders who embrace feedback as an opportunity for growth set a powerful example for their team.

1. Stay Open-Minded

Resist the urge to become defensive or dismissive, even if the feedback stings. Focus on understanding the perspective of the person giving it.

> *Example*: If a team member says, "I feel like you don't always listen during our one-on-ones," don't respond with, "That's not true." Instead, say, "I didn't realize I was coming across that way. Can you share an example so I can understand better?"

2. Ask Questions

Clarify feedback to ensure you fully understand it. Questions like "What specific behaviors are you referring to?" or "How can I improve in this area?" show that you value their input.

3. Reflect Before Reacting

It's natural to feel defensive when receiving critical feedback. Take time to reflect before responding. This helps you process the feedback objectively and consider how to act on it.

4. Act on Feedback

Feedback is useless if it doesn't lead to change. Demonstrating that you've taken feedback seriously—whether by improving your behavior or implementing a new approach—builds trust and credibility.

Building a Feedback Culture

As a leader, it's your responsibility to create an environment where feedback flows freely in all directions. This requires fostering trust, normalizing feedback, and setting the tone for open communication.

1. Normalize Feedback

Make feedback a regular part of team interactions, not just something reserved for formal reviews.

- Incorporate feedback into weekly check-ins or project debriefs.
- Encourage team members to give feedback to each other.

2. Lead by Example

Be transparent about the feedback you receive and how you're acting on it. This shows your team that feedback is valuable, not something to fear.

> *Example*: Share with your team: "In my last 360 review, I got feedback that I sometimes dominate conversations. I've been working on pausing more and asking for others' input."

3. Recognize and Reinforce Positive Behavior

Create a habit of acknowledging good work and calling out positive behaviors. Public recognition can motivate the entire team to strive for excellence.

> *Example*: During a team meeting, say, "I want to thank Alex for going above and beyond to meet last week's deadline. Your extra effort really made a difference."

Practical Exercises for Feedback Mastery

Exercise 1: Feedback Self-Assessment

- Reflect on your recent feedback conversations:
    1. Was the feedback specific and actionable?
    2. Did you balance positive and constructive feedback?
    3. How did the recipient respond?
- Write down one thing you'll improve in your next feedback session.

Exercise 2: Role-Playing Feedback Conversations

- Pair with a colleague or friend to practice giving feedback. Use the Feedback Formula:
    1. State the situation.
    2. Describe the behavior.
    3. Explain the impact.
    4. Offer suggestions for improvement.
- Switch roles to practice receiving feedback with an open mind.

Exercise 3: Create a Feedback Plan

- Choose one team member and write out a feedback plan:
    1. What positive behaviors will you reinforce?
    2. What area for improvement will you address?
    3. How will you deliver the feedback? (e.g., one-on-one, during a project debrief)

Closing Thought: Feedback as a Catalyst for Growth

Feedback is not just a tool for correcting mistakes—it's a way to unlock potential, inspire growth, and build stronger relationships. As a leader, your ability to give and receive feedback with clarity and care will set the tone for your team's success.

Remember, feedback is a gift. It's an opportunity to help others improve and to improve yourself in the process. When feedback becomes a natural, ongoing part of your leadership style, you'll create a culture where everyone strives to be their best—including you.

Chapter 8: Managing Conflict: Turning Tension into Collaboration

Introduction: Why Conflict is Inevitable—and Necessary

Conflict. The word itself often makes people uncomfortable, especially in a workplace setting. Many leaders strive to avoid it, believing harmony is the key to productivity. But the truth is, conflict is inevitable when people with different perspectives, goals, and personalities work together.

In fact, conflict isn't inherently bad. When managed well, it can spark creativity, improve decision-making, and strengthen relationships. It's through healthy disagreements that teams often find the best solutions and push each other to grow. The key lies not in avoiding conflict but in addressing it constructively.

As a manager, you're not just a bystander when tensions arise—you're responsible for guiding your team through them. Whether it's a heated argument between colleagues, miscommunication across departments, or unspoken frustrations bubbling under the surface, your ability to navigate conflict will determine whether it strengthens or weakens your team.

This chapter will show you how to:

1. Recognize the types of conflict that arise in teams.
2. Manage interpersonal tension with empathy and fairness.
3. Prevent small issues from escalating into larger problems.
4. Turn disagreements into opportunities for growth and collaboration.

Great leaders don't shy away from conflict—they lean into it with confidence and a mindset of resolution. Let's explore how you can do the same.

Section 1: Understanding the Types of Conflict

Not all conflicts are the same, and understanding their root causes will help you address them more effectively.

1. Task-Based Conflict

- **Definition**: Disagreements about *what* needs to be done or *how* it should be done.
- **Examples**: Differing opinions on project priorities, timelines, or approaches.
- **Potential Upside**: Task-based conflicts often lead to innovative solutions when handled constructively.

Scenario: Two team members argue over whether to prioritize product features for existing customers or focus on acquiring new ones. A resolution might involve reviewing data to align the team on what will deliver the greatest impact.

Case Study 1: Task-Based Conflict – The Marketing vs. Product Dispute

Scenario:

At a mid-sized software company, the marketing team and product development team are clashing over priorities for an upcoming product launch. Marketing wants to focus on features that will attract new customers, while the product team believes it's more important to address feedback from existing users to reduce churn. Each team feels their perspective is being ignored, and the disagreement is delaying progress.

Conflict Type: Task-Based Conflict

Action Taken:

The manager brings both teams together for a facilitated discussion.

1. **Listening to both sides**: Each team presents their case, focusing on data and objectives.

2. **Finding common ground**: The manager reframes the conflict, saying, "Both teams want the product to succeed, and both priorities—new customers and retention—are important."
3. **Collaborative solution**: They agree to launch with a balance of new features and improved user experience. Marketing gets to highlight new features, while the product team addresses customer feedback in a later update.

Outcome:

The teams walk away feeling heard and aligned. The project progresses with renewed collaboration, and the launch meets both new customer acquisition and retention goals.

Key Lesson:

Task-based conflicts can often be resolved by identifying shared goals and creating a plan that balances competing priorities.

2. Relationship-Based Conflict

- **Definition**: Personal tensions stemming from personality clashes, misunderstandings, or emotional triggers.
- **Examples**: One team member perceives another as dismissive or controlling, leading to ongoing resentment.
- **Potential Downside**: These conflicts can damage team cohesion if left unresolved.

Scenario: A team member feels micromanaged by a colleague and starts avoiding collaboration. This requires a direct conversation to clarify intentions and reset expectations.

Case Study 2: Relationship-Based Conflict – Personality Clashes

Scenario:
Two team members, Sarah and Tom, are constantly butting heads. Sarah perceives Tom's direct

communication style as rude, while Tom feels Sarah is overly sensitive and avoids addressing problems directly. Their tension is disrupting team dynamics and making meetings uncomfortable.

Conflict Type: Relationship-Based Conflict

Action Taken:

The manager intervenes with a mediation session:

1. **Private conversations**: The manager meets with each person individually to understand their concerns. Sarah explains she feels dismissed by Tom's tone, and Tom shares his frustration with what he sees as a lack of transparency.
2. **Facilitating dialogue**: In a joint meeting, the manager sets ground rules for respectful communication and asks each person to explain their perspective. The manager encourages both parties to reframe their assumptions about the other's intentions.
3. **Finding a path forward**: Sarah and Tom agree to give each other feedback constructively and

commit to addressing misunderstandings in the moment rather than letting frustrations build.

Outcome:

Over time, Sarah and Tom learn to work together more effectively. Their improved relationship boosts team morale and eliminates distractions caused by their conflict.

Key Lesson:

Relationship-based conflicts often stem from miscommunication and assumptions. A facilitated conversation can help uncover underlying issues and reset expectations.

3. Role-Based Conflict

- **Definition**: Confusion or disagreements about roles, responsibilities, or authority.
- **Examples**: Two team members believing they're responsible for the same task—or no one taking responsibility for a key deliverable.

- **Solution**: Clarifying roles and decision-making authority prevents recurring tensions.

Scenario: In a cross-functional project, the marketing team and product team argue over who owns messaging for a campaign. A leader can resolve this by clearly defining ownership and collaboration points.

Case Study 3: Role-Based Conflict – The Ownership Overlap

Scenario:

During a cross-functional project, Jessica from operations and Alex from logistics both assume they're responsible for finalizing vendor contracts. Jessica moves forward without consulting Alex, who feels excluded and undermined. This leads to duplicate work, missed deadlines, and mounting frustration between the two.

Conflict Type: Role-Based Conflict

Action Taken:

The manager steps in to clarify roles and responsibilities:

1. **Acknowledging the conflict**: The manager calls a meeting with both Jessica and Alex, acknowledging the confusion and frustrations.
2. **Clarifying ownership**: The manager outlines a clear division of responsibilities: Jessica will handle initial vendor outreach, while Alex will finalize contracts. They will collaborate during key milestones to ensure alignment.
3. **Establishing processes**: The manager introduces a shared project plan with clear timelines and responsibilities, reducing the risk of future overlap.

Outcome:

With clear roles established, Jessica and Alex move forward without further conflict. The project is completed on time, and both feel their contributions are valued.

Key Lesson:
Role-based conflicts often stem from ambiguity. Clarifying ownership and creating shared processes can prevent misunderstandings and improve collaboration.

Section 2: The Cost of Avoiding Conflict

Ignoring conflict doesn't make it go away—it often makes it worse. Left unaddressed, small disagreements can fester into larger, more disruptive issues that harm morale and productivity.

Signs of Unresolved Conflict:

- Passive-aggressive behavior, like withholding information or cooperation.
- Decreased communication between team members.
- A toxic atmosphere where people avoid speaking up.
- Poor performance or missed deadlines due to lack of collaboration.

Example: A manager notices tension between two employees but avoids addressing it directly. Over time, their refusal to work together affects team performance, forcing the manager to step in when the problem has escalated.

Key Lesson: Addressing conflict early—before it spirals—is one of the most effective ways to maintain trust and productivity within your team.

Case Study 4: Avoiding Conflict – The Snowball Effect

Scenario:
At a growing startup, two team members, Priya and James, have been quietly at odds for weeks. Priya feels James isn't pulling his weight on a shared project, while James believes Priya is overstepping by taking control of tasks he's responsible for. Instead of addressing the tension, both avoid direct communication, leading to a toxic dynamic.

Conflict Type: Relationship-Based Conflict Escalated by Avoidance

Action Taken:

The manager notices the deteriorating relationship and intervenes before it disrupts the project further:

1. **One-on-one check-ins**: The manager meets separately with Priya and James to understand their frustrations. Both admit they've been avoiding a direct conversation about their concerns.
2. **Facilitating a resolution**: The manager brings them together for a structured discussion, encouraging them to focus on behaviors rather than blaming each other. Priya explains she's felt the need to take over because deadlines are slipping, while James shares that Priya's micromanagement has made him disengage.
3. **Collaborative problem-solving**: They agree to reassign specific tasks, set clearer expectations, and schedule weekly check-ins to align progress.

Outcome:

With open communication restored, Priya and James rebuild their working relationship. Their productivity improves, and the project is delivered successfully.

Key Lesson:

Avoiding conflict doesn't resolve it—it often makes it worse. Addressing tensions early prevents issues from escalating and allows for faster resolution.

Section 3: How to Manage Conflict Effectively

1. Approach Conflict with Empathy

Conflict often stems from unmet needs or misunderstood perspectives. By approaching disagreements with empathy, you can uncover the root cause and foster mutual understanding.

- **How to practice empathy**:
    - Listen actively and without interruption.
    - Acknowledge the emotions involved.

- Ask open-ended questions to understand each person's perspective.

Example: In a disagreement about workload distribution, say, "I can see that you're feeling overwhelmed. Let's talk about what's contributing to that and how we can adjust the workload."

2. Focus on the Problem, Not the Person

It's easy for disagreements to feel personal, but focusing on behaviors and solutions keeps the conversation productive.

- **How to stay objective**:
    - Avoid blaming language ("You always…") and focus on the issue at hand.
    - Reframe accusations as shared challenges.
    - Use "I" statements to express concerns.

Example: Instead of saying, "You're unreliable with deadlines," say, "I noticed the last two deadlines were missed. Let's figure out what's causing the delays and how we can address it."

3. Facilitate Open Dialogue

When tensions are high, your role as a leader is to create a safe space for both sides to share their perspectives.

- **Steps to facilitate**:
    1. Bring the parties together in a neutral setting.
    2. Set ground rules for respectful communication.
    3. Allow each person to share their perspective without interruption.
    4. Identify common ground and focus on shared goals.

    Example: Two team members disagree over resource allocation. As the leader, you can guide the conversation by saying, "Let's start by each sharing what's most important to you in this situation. Then we'll explore how to balance those needs."

4. Follow Up After Resolution

Conflict resolution doesn't end with a single conversation. Following up ensures the agreement is being honored and prevents misunderstandings from resurfacing.

- **How to follow up effectively**:
    - Check in with both parties a week or two later to see how things are going.
    - Reiterate any changes or agreements that were made.
    - Offer additional support if needed.

Example: After resolving a disagreement about task ownership, you could follow up by saying, "How are things going with the new process we discussed? Is there anything else we need to adjust?"

Section 4: Turning Conflict into Collaboration

1. Reframe Conflict as Opportunity

When handled well, conflict can lead to stronger relationships and better outcomes. Use disagreements as a chance to:

- Explore new ideas and perspectives.
- Identify and address underlying issues.
- Build trust by showing fairness and empathy.

Example: A heated debate about a product feature might lead to a breakthrough idea that combines both perspectives into a better solution.

Task-Based Conflict Section:

"To see how task-based conflicts play out in real teams, let's look at a situation involving competing priorities between two departments."

Case Study 1: Task-Based Conflict – The Marketing vs. Product Dispute

Scenario:

At a mid-sized software company, the marketing team and product development team are clashing over priorities for an upcoming product launch. Marketing wants to focus on features that will attract new customers, while the product team believes it's more important to address feedback from existing users to reduce churn. Each team feels their perspective is being ignored, and the disagreement is delaying progress.

Conflict Type: Task-Based Conflict

Action Taken:

The manager brings both teams together for a facilitated discussion.

1. **Listening to both sides**: Each team presents their case, focusing on data and objectives.

2. **Finding common ground**: The manager reframes the conflict, saying, "Both teams want the product to succeed, and both priorities—new customers and retention—are important."
3. **Collaborative solution**: They agree to launch with a balance of new features and improved user experience. Marketing gets to highlight new features, while the product team addresses customer feedback in a later update.

Outcome:
The teams walk away feeling heard and aligned. The project progresses with renewed collaboration, and the launch meets both new customer acquisition and retention goals.

Key Lesson:
Task-based conflicts can often be resolved by identifying shared goals and creating a plan that balances competing priorities.

Relationship-Based Conflict Section:

"Here's an example of a personality clash that disrupted team harmony—and how it was resolved."

Case Study 2: Relationship-Based Conflict – Personality Clashes

Scenario:

Two team members, Sarah and Tom, are constantly butting heads. Sarah perceives Tom's direct communication style as rude, while Tom feels Sarah is overly sensitive and avoids addressing problems directly. Their tension is disrupting team dynamics and making meetings uncomfortable.

Conflict Type: Relationship-Based Conflict

Action Taken:

The manager intervenes with a mediation session:

1. **Private conversations**: The manager meets with each person individually to understand their

concerns. Sarah explains she feels dismissed by Tom's tone, and Tom shares his frustration with what he sees as a lack of transparency.
2. **Facilitating dialogue**: In a joint meeting, the manager sets ground rules for respectful communication and asks each person to explain their perspective. The manager encourages both parties to reframe their assumptions about the other's intentions.
3. **Finding a path forward**: Sarah and Tom agree to give each other feedback constructively and commit to addressing misunderstandings in the moment rather than letting frustrations build.

Outcome:
Over time, Sarah and Tom learn to work together more effectively. Their improved relationship boosts team morale and eliminates distractions caused by their conflict.

Key Lesson:
Relationship-based conflicts often stem from

miscommunication and assumptions. A facilitated conversation can help uncover underlying issues and reset expectations.

Role-Based Conflict Section:

> "Role-based conflicts often arise when responsibilities overlap. The following case study demonstrates how clarifying ownership can resolve tensions."

Case Study 3: Role-Based Conflict – The Ownership Overlap

Scenario:
During a cross-functional project, Jessica from operations and Alex from logistics both assume they're responsible for finalizing vendor contracts. Jessica moves forward without consulting Alex, who feels excluded and undermined. This leads to duplicate work,

missed deadlines, and mounting frustration between the two.

Conflict Type: Role-Based Conflict

Action Taken:
The manager steps in to clarify roles and responsibilities:

1. **Acknowledging the conflict**: The manager calls a meeting with both Jessica and Alex, acknowledging the confusion and frustrations.
2. **Clarifying ownership**: The manager outlines a clear division of responsibilities: Jessica will handle initial vendor outreach, while Alex will finalize contracts. They will collaborate during key milestones to ensure alignment.
3. **Establishing processes**: The manager introduces a shared project plan with clear timelines and responsibilities, reducing the risk of future overlap.

Outcome:
With clear roles established, Jessica and Alex move

forward without further conflict. The project is completed on time, and both feel their contributions are valued.

Key Lesson:
Role-based conflicts often stem from ambiguity. Clarifying ownership and creating shared processes can prevent misunderstandings and improve collaboration.

Cost of Avoiding Conflict Section:

> "Avoiding conflict often leads to greater issues. This case study shows how ignoring small tensions can spiral into a larger problem."

Case Study 4: Avoiding Conflict – The Snowball Effect

Scenario:
At a growing startup, two team members, Priya and James, have been quietly at odds for weeks. Priya feels

James isn't pulling his weight on a shared project, while James believes Priya is overstepping by taking control of tasks he's responsible for. Instead of addressing the tension, both avoid direct communication, leading to a toxic dynamic.

Conflict Type: Relationship-Based Conflict Escalated by Avoidance

Action Taken:
The manager notices the deteriorating relationship and intervenes before it disrupts the project further:

1. **One-on-one check-ins**: The manager meets separately with Priya and James to understand their frustrations. Both admit they've been avoiding a direct conversation about their concerns.
2. **Facilitating a resolution**: The manager brings them together for a structured discussion, encouraging them to focus on behaviors rather than blaming each other. Priya explains she's felt the need to take over because deadlines are

slipping, while James shares that Priya's micromanagement has made him disengage.
3. **Collaborative problem-solving**: They agree to reassign specific tasks, set clearer expectations, and schedule weekly check-ins to align progress.

Outcome:

With open communication restored, Priya and James rebuild their working relationship. Their productivity improves, and the project is delivered successfully.

Key Lesson:

Avoiding conflict doesn't resolve it—it often makes it worse. Addressing tensions early prevents issues from escalating and allows for faster resolution.

Turning Conflict into Collaboration Section:

> "Conflict doesn't have to be destructive. The following example illustrates how tension between two team members led to a breakthrough innovation."

Case Study 5: Reframing Conflict – Turning Tension into Innovation

Scenario:

During a product brainstorming session, two team members, Emily and Raj, have starkly different ideas about the product's direction. Emily wants to pursue a minimalist design, while Raj advocates for a feature-rich approach. The disagreement becomes heated, with both digging in their heels.

Conflict Type: Task-Based Conflict with High Stakes

Action Taken:

The manager reframes the conflict as an opportunity for collaboration:

1. **Encouraging diverse perspectives**: The manager points out that both ideas have merit and asks the team to explore ways to integrate the best elements of each.

2. **Collaborative exploration**: Emily and Raj work together to develop prototypes that balance simplicity with functionality.
3. **Data-driven decision-making**: The team conducts user testing to gather feedback on both approaches, ultimately landing on a hybrid design that satisfies both priorities.

Outcome:

The final product receives rave reviews for its balance of simplicity and features, and Emily and Raj develop mutual respect through their collaboration.

Key Lesson:

Conflict over ideas can lead to innovation when approached with curiosity and a willingness to explore new possibilities.

2. Teach Conflict Management Skills to Your Team

Empowering your team to resolve conflicts independently reduces your workload and fosters a more collaborative culture.

- **How to teach these skills**:
    - Role-play common conflict scenarios during team meetings.
    - Encourage team members to address small disagreements directly with each other.
    - Provide resources, like books or workshops, on communication and conflict resolution.

Practical Exercises for Managing Conflict

Exercise 1: Conflict Reflection

1. Think of a recent conflict on your team (or in your own experience).
2. Reflect on:
    - What caused the conflict?
    - How was it resolved (or not resolved)?

- What could have been done differently?

Exercise 2: Role-Playing Conflict Resolution

1. Pair up with a colleague or team member.
2. Role-play a conflict scenario, with one person acting as the mediator.
3. Practice using empathy, active listening, and problem-solving to reach a resolution.

Exercise 3: Prevention Planning

1. Identify potential sources of conflict in your team (e.g., unclear roles, workload distribution).
2. Create a plan to address these proactively, such as clarifying expectations or scheduling regular check-ins.

Closing Thought: Embracing Conflict as a Leadership Skill

Conflict is an inevitable part of leadership, but it doesn't have to be a source of fear or frustration. When handled effectively, it's an opportunity to strengthen your team, improve communication, and drive better results.

Remember, conflict isn't about "winning" or "losing." It's about creating understanding, finding common ground, and moving forward together. By embracing conflict as a natural part of collaboration—and equipping yourself with the skills to manage it—you'll foster a culture of trust, innovation, and resilience.

So, the next time tension arises, don't avoid it. Lean into the discomfort, listen deeply, and lead your team toward resolution. With practice, you'll turn every conflict into an opportunity for growth.

Chapter 9: Managing Up: Building Strong Relationships with Your Boss

Leadership isn't just about managing your team—it's also about effectively managing your relationship with your boss. While much of leadership training focuses on guiding your team, equally important is the ability to **align upward** with your direct supervisor or senior leadership. Whether you work in a startup or a multinational corporation, your success is closely tied to your ability to understand and align with your boss's priorities, goals, and expectations.

Managing up is not about flattery or manipulation. It's about building a **productive, mutually beneficial partnership** where both you and your boss succeed. It's about taking ownership of your role, anticipating needs, and finding ways to make your boss's job easier. When you manage up effectively, you're not just positioning yourself for success—you're also improving outcomes for your team and your organization.

Why Managing Up Matters

Your boss is a critical link between you and the broader organization. They set the tone for your team, advocate for resources, and influence decisions that affect your success. When you align with your boss and manage that relationship well, you:

- **Ensure your team's priorities align with organizational goals**: A well-aligned relationship ensures you're working on the right things, avoiding miscommunication or wasted effort.
- **Reduce friction and misunderstandings**: Clear communication minimizes confusion and allows your team to operate more efficiently.
- **Build trust and credibility**: When your boss trusts you to deliver results and solve problems independently, you gain more autonomy and opportunities.

Why People Hesitate to Manage Up

Many managers hesitate to actively "manage up" because they fear it may come across as self-serving or political. Some worry it might feel like they're pandering or trying to curry favor with their boss. But this hesitation often stems from a misunderstanding of what managing up really is.

Managing up isn't about being a "yes person" or blindly agreeing with your boss. Instead, it's about creating alignment, fostering collaboration, and finding ways to support your boss in achieving their goals while still advocating for your own team. Done right, it's a win-win.

> *Think of managing up as strategic communication, not flattery. It's about ensuring you and your boss are rowing in the same direction to achieve shared goals.*

How Managing Up Benefits Everyone

When done effectively, managing up creates a ripple effect of positive outcomes:

1. **Your Boss Benefits**: You become a trusted partner they can rely on, helping them achieve their goals with less stress and effort.
2. **Your Team Benefits**: A strong relationship with your boss ensures your team has the resources, support, and clarity it needs to thrive.
3. **You Benefit**: By demonstrating reliability, initiative, and strategic thinking, you position yourself as a valuable leader worthy of increased trust, autonomy, and growth opportunities.

What This Chapter Will Teach You

In this chapter, you'll learn how to:

1. **Understand your boss's unique goals, priorities, and communication style.** No two bosses are the same, and adapting to their

preferences is key to building a strong relationship.
2. **Communicate effectively and proactively.** Learn how to keep your boss informed, raise challenges with solutions, and provide value in every interaction.
3. **Build trust and credibility.** Gain the tools to demonstrate reliability and solve problems before they reach your boss's desk.
4. **Handle misalignment or conflict constructively.** Learn how to navigate disagreements or differing priorities without damaging the relationship.

A Leadership Mindset: Managing Up as a Partnership

Your relationship with your boss is one of the most important professional relationships you'll have. It's not just about following orders or completing tasks—it's about fostering trust, collaboration, and alignment. By managing up effectively, you demonstrate leadership in its truest form: creating connections, solving problems, and ensuring that everyone—from your team to your boss to yourself—can succeed.

Let's dive into the strategies, tools, and techniques you'll need to make this relationship strong, strategic, and mutually beneficial.

Section 1: Understanding Your Boss's Needs and Goals

To manage up effectively, you need to understand your boss's unique preferences, priorities, and expectations. Every leader has their own style, and part of your job is to adapt to it.

1. Identify Their Priorities

Your boss's priorities likely align with the organization's broader goals. Understanding these priorities will help you focus your efforts on what matters most to them.

- **How to identify priorities**:

- Pay attention to what they emphasize in meetings.
- Observe where they allocate their time and resources.
- Ask directly: *"What are your top priorities for our team this quarter?"*

Example: If your boss is focused on reducing costs, emphasize how your team's efforts align with budget optimization in your updates.

2. Learn Their Communication Style

Some leaders prefer detailed reports, while others want high-level summaries. Adapting to your boss's preferred communication style shows you're attentive and makes your interactions more efficient.

- **Key styles to look for**:
  - **Detail-oriented**: They prefer data, reports, and specific metrics.

- **Big-picture focused**: They want key takeaways and implications, not granular details.
- **Hands-on**: They like to be involved in day-to-day decisions.
- **Delegator**: They prefer to set broad goals and let you take the lead.

Tip: Pay attention to how your boss communicates—do they send lengthy emails or brief messages? Mirror their style to make your communication more effective.

3. Anticipate Their Needs

Great leaders solve problems before they reach their boss's desk. Anticipating what your boss will need—whether it's data for an upcoming presentation or a heads-up about a potential issue—makes you an indispensable partner.

- **How to anticipate needs**:

- Stay aware of upcoming deadlines, meetings, and projects.
- Think a step ahead: *"What will my boss need to succeed in this situation?"*
- Flag potential problems early, along with possible solutions.

Example: If you know your boss is presenting to the executive team next week, prepare a concise report summarizing key updates from your team.

Section 2: Communicating Effectively with Your Boss

Communication is the foundation of any strong relationship, including the one you have with your boss. Knowing how to communicate clearly, professionally, and constructively will strengthen trust and collaboration.

1. Provide Regular Updates

Keep your boss informed about your team's progress, challenges, and results. Regular updates prevent surprises and show you're proactive.

- **Best practices**:
    - Use weekly email summaries or one-on-one meetings to share progress.
    - Highlight achievements, but don't shy away from discussing challenges.

    Example: "This week, we completed the first phase of the project on schedule. One challenge we're encountering is delays in vendor responses—I'm working with Alex to resolve this and will keep you posted."

2. Frame Challenges with Solutions

When raising a problem, always come prepared with potential solutions. This demonstrates critical thinking and reduces the burden on your boss to "fix" the issue.

- **How to frame challenges**:
    1. State the issue clearly.

2. Explain the potential impact.
3. Offer 1–2 potential solutions.

Example: "We're facing a delay in the client approval process, which might push the project timeline back by a week. To address this, we could either reallocate resources to speed up other phases or request additional client meetings to clarify expectations."

3. Seek and Use Feedback

Actively ask your boss for feedback on your performance and your team's progress. Then, implement that feedback to show you value their input.

- **Questions to ask**:
    - *"What's one thing I could do differently to make your job easier?"*
    - *"Are there any adjustments you'd like me to make in how I'm leading the team?"*

Tip: Don't just ask for feedback—act on it and let your boss know how you're applying it.

Section 3: Building Trust and Credibility

Trust and credibility are the foundation of managing up successfully. Your boss needs to know they can rely on you to deliver results, act with integrity, and make their job easier.

1. Be Reliable

Follow through on your commitments and consistently deliver high-quality work. Reliability builds trust over time.

Example: If you commit to providing a report by Friday, deliver it on time—every time.

2. Share Credit Generously

Highlight the contributions of your team and give credit where it's due. Leaders who share credit earn the respect of both their boss and their team.

> *Example*: In a meeting, say, "The success of this project is thanks to Sarah's outstanding data analysis and the support of the entire team."

3. Stay Solution-Oriented

Leaders who focus on solving problems, rather than dwelling on them, demonstrate maturity and competence.

Section 4: Navigating Misalignment or Conflict with Your Boss

No matter how strong your relationship with your boss is, there will be times when you disagree. Learning to handle misalignment constructively is a key part of managing up.

1. Focus on Shared Goals

Disagreements often arise from differing approaches, not opposing objectives. Reframe the conversation by focusing on shared goals.

> *Example*: "I understand you want to reduce costs, and I want to ensure we maintain quality. Let's explore ways to achieve both."

2. Choose Your Battles

Not every disagreement needs to be escalated. Focus on the issues that truly matter and let smaller disagreements go.

> *Tip*: Before pushing back, ask yourself, *"Does this decision impact the long-term success of the team or the project?"*

3. Use Data to Support Your Case

When presenting a differing perspective, back it up with data or examples. This makes your argument more objective and less emotional.

Example: Instead of saying, "I think we need more resources," say, "With current staffing levels, we're projected to miss the deadline by two weeks. Adding one more

Practical Exercises for Managing Up

Exercise 1: Boss Profile

- Write down:
    - Your boss's top 3 priorities.
    - Their preferred communication style.
    - Their biggest challenges.
- Reflect on how your work aligns with these areas and identify adjustments you can make.

Exercise 2: Proactive Problem-Solving

- Think of a recent challenge your boss had to solve.
- Write down:
    - How you could have anticipated the problem.
    - What solutions you could have provided.

- Use this as a template for handling future challenges.

Closing Thought: A Partnership for Success

Your relationship with your boss isn't just about hierarchy—it's a partnership. Managing up effectively creates alignment, reduces friction, and ultimately benefits your entire team. By understanding your boss's needs, communicating proactively, and building trust through reliability and results, you'll strengthen this relationship and position yourself as a valued leader.

Remember, managing up isn't about being a "yes person." It's about building a collaborative partnership where both you and your boss succeed. Approach this relationship with curiosity, respect, and a solution-oriented mindset, and you'll unlock opportunities for growth—for yourself, your boss, and your team.

Chapter 10: Time Management for Leaders: Balancing Priorities in a Demanding Role

Introduction: The Leadership Time Trap

One of the most challenging transitions for new managers is learning how to manage time effectively in a role that comes with endless demands. You're not only responsible for your own workload but also for leading your team, meeting organizational goals, and addressing the unexpected issues that arise daily. Suddenly, your to-do list feels infinite, and there's never enough time in the day to do it all.

Time management as a leader isn't just about working harder or longer hours. It's about **working smarter**—balancing priorities, delegating effectively, and protecting time for the things that matter most. It's also about recognizing that your role as a manager requires a different mindset: success is no longer measured by how much you personally accomplish but by how well you guide your team to achieve collective goals.

This chapter will equip you with tools and strategies to:

1. Identify and prioritize your most important tasks.

2. Delegate effectively to free up time for leadership and strategic work.
3. Manage interruptions and stay focused in a fast-paced environment.
4. Protect time for personal development and avoid burnout.

Leadership is as much about managing yourself as it is about managing others. Let's dive into the principles of time management that will help you lead more effectively while maintaining balance.

Section 1: Rethinking Time Management as a Leader

As a leader, time management isn't just about being productive—it's about aligning your time with your **highest-value activities**.

1. Your Time Is a Resource

Every minute you spend on low-value tasks is a minute you're not spending on leadership priorities. Think of your time as a resource to be invested wisely.

- **High-value activities**: Strategic planning, coaching your team, solving critical problems, building relationships, and making decisions that drive results.
- **Low-value activities**: Administrative work, micromanaging, attending unnecessary meetings, or doing tasks that could be delegated.

Tip: At the start of each week, ask yourself, *"Am I spending my time where I can make the greatest impact?"*

2. Success Isn't About Doing It All

It's tempting to think that working harder and saying "yes" to everything will make you a great leader. But in reality, spreading yourself too thin often leads to poor results, burnout, and frustration for your team.

- **Key mindset shift**: Stop trying to do it all. Focus on doing the most important things well.

3. The Leadership "Priority Shift"

As a leader, your priorities shift from completing tasks yourself to:

1. **Guiding your team**: Spending time on coaching, problem-solving, and empowering others.
2. **Thinking strategically**: Allocating time to long-term planning and big-picture thinking.
3. **Building relationships**: Strengthening connections with your team, peers, and leadership.

Example: Instead of spending hours perfecting a report, delegate it to a team member and use that time to prepare for an important meeting with senior leadership.

Section 2: Strategies for Effective Time Management

1. Prioritize Ruthlessly

Not all tasks are created equal. Prioritizing effectively means identifying the activities that have the greatest impact on your goals and focusing your energy there.

- **The Eisenhower Matrix**: Categorize tasks into four quadrants:
    - **Urgent and Important**: Do these immediately.
    - **Important but Not Urgent**: Schedule these.
    - **Urgent but Not Important**: Delegate these.
    - **Neither Urgent nor Important**: Eliminate these.

    Example: Instead of reacting to every email, set aside time to focus on high-impact tasks like planning team strategy or coaching a struggling team member.

2. Master the Art of Delegation

Leaders who try to do everything themselves become bottlenecks for their team. Delegating effectively frees up your time while developing your team's skills.

- **What to delegate**: Tasks that others can do as well—or better—than you, or tasks that help team members grow.
- **What not to delegate**: High-level decision-making, sensitive conversations, and tasks critical to your leadership role.

Tip: If you're reluctant to delegate, remember that delegation is an investment in your team's development—and your sanity.

3. Schedule Time for Strategic Thinking

As a leader, it's easy to get consumed by day-to-day tasks and neglect long-term planning. Protecting time for strategic thinking allows you to anticipate challenges, set goals, and align your team's efforts with the bigger picture.

- **How to schedule it**: Block out 1–2 hours each week for uninterrupted strategic work. Treat this time as sacred—no meetings, no distractions.

Example: Use your strategic thinking time to review your team's progress, identify potential roadblocks, and plan for the next quarter.

4. Manage Interruptions and Stay Focused

Interruptions are a fact of life for leaders. Learning how to minimize them and stay focused on your priorities is essential.

- **How to manage interruptions**:
    - Set "office hours" for team questions and concerns.
    - Use tools like email autoresponders to let people know when you'll respond.
    - Politely decline unnecessary meetings or delegate your attendance when appropriate.

Example: If a team member frequently interrupts with non-urgent questions, schedule a daily check-in to address their concerns all at once.

Section 3: Protecting Your Energy and Avoiding Burnout

1. Recognize the Signs of Burnout

Burnout doesn't happen overnight—it builds slowly over time. As a leader, it's critical to recognize the signs and take action before it impacts your performance or well-being.

- **Common signs**:
    - Feeling constantly overwhelmed or exhausted.
    - Losing enthusiasm for work.
    - Struggling to focus or make decisions.

Tip: Pay attention to your energy levels and don't ignore the warning signs.

2. Set Boundaries

Leaders often feel pressured to be "always on," but setting boundaries is key to maintaining balance.

- **How to set boundaries**:
    - Establish work hours and stick to them.
    - Turn off email notifications outside of work hours.
    - Communicate your boundaries to your team and boss.

    Example: Let your team know that you won't respond to emails after 6 p.m. unless it's an emergency.

3. Make Time for Personal Development

Great leaders don't just invest in their teams—they invest in themselves. Prioritize time for learning, reflection, and growth to stay sharp and inspired.

- **Ways to develop yourself**:

- Read books or listen to podcasts about leadership and industry trends.
- Attend conferences or workshops.
- Set aside time for reflection to evaluate your leadership and identify areas for improvement.

Tip: Schedule at least one hour a week for personal development, whether it's reading, networking, or taking a course.

Practical Exercises for Time Management

Exercise 1: The Time Audit

1. Track how you spend your time for one week.
2. Categorize your activities as high-value, low-value, or wasted time.
3. Identify at least three activities you can delegate or eliminate.

Exercise 2: Build Your Ideal Week

1. Create a weekly calendar template that reflects your ideal time allocation.
   - Include blocks for strategic thinking, team check-ins, and personal development.
2. Compare it to your current schedule and make adjustments to align with your priorities.

Exercise 3: The Delegation Challenge

1. Identify one task you've been reluctant to delegate.
2. Choose a team member who could handle it and develop a delegation plan.
3. Reflect on the results after delegating the task.

Closing Thought: Leading with Time on Your Side

Time is the one resource you can never create more of, but as a leader, how you choose to invest your time determines your impact, your success, and your well-being. Leadership is not about squeezing as much as possible into your day; it's about focusing your energy on what truly matters. The way you manage your time directly affects your ability to lead effectively, inspire your team, and achieve meaningful results.

When you prioritize your highest-value activities—such as coaching your team, thinking strategically, and building relationships—you create a ripple effect of positive outcomes. Your team will have clearer guidance, stronger support, and more room to grow under your leadership. Your organization will benefit from your focus on long-term goals and well-executed priorities. And most importantly, you'll protect your own energy and avoid the burnout that so often accompanies a fast-paced managerial role.

But time management is about more than just efficiency—it's a reflection of your leadership values. The way you allocate your time sends a message to your team about what you consider important. If you spend too much time on busywork or micromanaging, you inadvertently tell your team that you don't trust them. When you focus on strategy, empowerment, and personal development, you signal that growth, trust, and results are what matter most.

Mastering time management also allows you to embrace a critical aspect of leadership: **balance**. You can't give your best to your team or your organization if you're running on empty. Setting boundaries, prioritizing self-care, and carving out time for personal growth aren't selfish—they're essential. A well-rested, focused leader is far more effective than one who's perpetually overwhelmed.

Finally, remember that time management is a journey, not a one-time fix. It requires consistent reflection, adjustments, and discipline. You'll need to regularly assess how you're spending your time, delegate more as your team grows, and reprioritize as new challenges arise. The good news? Every step you take toward better time management will compound over time, making you not just a more productive leader, but a more effective, inspiring one.

"Leadership isn't about doing more—it's about doing what matters most."

As you move forward, ask yourself these key questions each week:

1. Am I spending my time on the activities that create the most value?
2. What can I delegate to empower my team and free up my energy for strategic priorities?
3. Am I protecting time for growth, reflection, and long-term planning?

By managing your time with intention, you'll lead with clarity, focus, and purpose—not just for your team, but for yourself as well. Time isn't just something to manage—it's the foundation for how you lead.

Now, take charge of your time. Your leadership depends on it.

Chapter 11: Emotional Intelligence in Leadership: Leading with Empathy and Awareness

Introduction: Why Emotional Intelligence Matters in Leadership

Think about the leaders you admire most. Chances are, they weren't just intelligent or skilled—they were emotionally intelligent. They were the kind of leaders who made you feel valued, understood, and motivated to do your best work.

Emotional intelligence (EQ) is one of the most important traits of an effective leader. It's what allows you to connect with your team, navigate difficult situations, and inspire trust. In today's workplace, where collaboration and relationships are key to success, EQ is no longer optional—it's essential.

As a leader, your ability to understand and manage your emotions directly impacts how you handle stress, communicate with your team, and make decisions. Equally important is your ability to recognize and respond to the emotions of others. When you lead with empathy and awareness, you create an environment where people feel supported, respected, and empowered to thrive.

This chapter will teach you how to:

1. Understand the five components of emotional intelligence.
2. Develop self-awareness and self-regulation to manage your emotions effectively.
3. Build stronger relationships with empathy and social awareness.
4. Handle emotionally charged situations with confidence and composure.

Leadership isn't just about what you do—it's about how you make people feel. Let's explore how emotional intelligence can transform your leadership and your team.

Section 1: The Five Components of Emotional Intelligence

Psychologist Daniel Goleman, who popularized the concept of emotional intelligence, identified five core components that are essential for effective leadership.

1. Self-Awareness

- **Definition**: The ability to recognize and understand your own emotions, as well as their impact on your thoughts and actions.
- **Why it matters**: Leaders who are self-aware can identify their emotional triggers and respond thoughtfully instead of reacting impulsively.

Example: A self-aware leader notices they're feeling frustrated during a meeting and pauses before speaking to avoid snapping at their team.

2. Self-Regulation

- **Definition**: The ability to control or redirect disruptive emotions and behaviors.
- **Why it matters**: Leaders who can regulate their emotions are better equipped to handle stress and stay calm under pressure.

Example: Instead of panicking when a project hits a major roadblock, a leader with strong self-regulation calmly assesses the situation and guides their team toward a solution.

3. Motivation

- **Definition**: The ability to stay focused on long-term goals and maintain a positive attitude, even in the face of setbacks.
- **Why it matters**: Leaders with intrinsic motivation inspire their teams by demonstrating

resilience and a commitment to achieving meaningful results.

Example: A motivated leader rallies their team after a failed product launch, using the experience as a learning opportunity to improve future efforts.

4. Empathy

- **Definition**: The ability to understand and share the feelings of others.
- **Why it matters**: Empathy allows leaders to build trust, foster collaboration, and address the needs of their team members effectively.

Example: An empathetic leader notices a team member is disengaged and takes the time to check in privately, discovering they're struggling with personal challenges.

5. Social Skills

- **Definition**: The ability to manage relationships, build networks, and communicate effectively.
- **Why it matters**: Strong social skills enable leaders to influence others, resolve conflicts, and create a positive team culture.

Example: A leader with strong social skills mediates a disagreement between team members, helping them find common ground and move forward productively.

Section 2: Developing Self-Awareness and Self-Regulation

1. Practicing Self-Awareness

Building self-awareness starts with reflection and observation.

- **Strategies**:
    - Keep a journal to track your emotions and how they influence your decisions.

- Ask for feedback from colleagues to gain insight into how others perceive your behavior.
- Pause regularly to check in with yourself: *"What am I feeling right now, and why?"*

2. Strengthening Self-Regulation

Managing your emotions effectively requires discipline and practice.

- **Strategies**:
  - Use mindfulness techniques, like deep breathing or meditation, to stay calm under pressure.
  - Reframe negative thoughts to focus on solutions instead of problems.
  - Practice delaying reactions—give yourself time to process your emotions before responding.

Section 3: Building Empathy and Social Awareness

1. Active Listening

Listening isn't just about hearing words—it's about understanding the emotions and perspectives behind them.

- **How to practice active listening**:
    - Maintain eye contact and avoid distractions during conversations.
    - Paraphrase what the other person says to confirm understanding.
    - Ask open-ended questions to encourage deeper dialogue.

2. Recognizing Nonverbal Cues

Much of communication is nonverbal. Paying attention to body language, tone of voice, and facial expressions helps you understand what people aren't saying.

> *Example*: A team member says they're "fine," but their slouched posture and lack of engagement suggest otherwise.

3. Showing Empathy

Empathy isn't about solving someone's problems—it's about showing you understand and care.

- **Strategies**:
    - Validate emotions: "I can see why you'd feel frustrated about this situation."
    - Be present: Show you're available to listen and support without judgment.

Section 4: Handling Emotionally Charged Situations

1. Stay Calm Under Pressure

As a leader, your team looks to you for stability. Remaining calm in high-stress situations helps you think clearly and reassures your team.

- **Strategies**:
    - Take a deep breath and focus on the facts of the situation.
    - Avoid escalating the tension—speak in a measured tone and avoid defensive language.

2. De-Escalate Conflicts

Emotionally charged conflicts require tact and emotional intelligence.

- **Steps to de-escalate**:
    1. Acknowledge emotions: "I can see this is a frustrating situation for you."
    2. Create space: Let each person express their perspective without interruption.
    3. Focus on solutions: Shift the conversation toward finding a resolution.

3. Rebuild Trust After Emotional Incidents

If an emotionally charged situation damages trust, it's important to repair the relationship.

- **Strategies**:
    - Apologize if necessary: "I realize my response came across as harsh. That wasn't my intention."
    - Follow up: Check in later to ensure the relationship is back on track.

Practical Exercises for Emotional Intelligence

Exercise 1: Emotional Triggers Journal

1. Identify situations that trigger strong emotional reactions.
2. Reflect on how you handled them and how you could respond more effectively in the future.

Exercise 2: Empathy Practice

1. Choose a team member to observe for a week.
2. Pay attention to their nonverbal cues and emotions during interactions.
3. Check in with them: "How are things going for you this week?"

Exercise 3: Conflict Role-Playing

1. Pair up with a colleague and role-play an emotionally charged scenario.
2. Practice staying calm, acknowledging emotions, and guiding the conversation toward resolution.

Closing Thought: Leading with Emotional Intelligence

Emotional intelligence isn't just a "nice-to-have" trait for leaders—it's the foundation that separates great leaders from average ones. Technical skills and strategic thinking might get you to a leadership role, but emotional intelligence is what helps you thrive in it. Leadership is fundamentally about people, and emotional intelligence is the bridge that connects you to those you lead, transforming workplace interactions into opportunities for growth, trust, and collaboration.

By mastering the five components of emotional intelligence—self-awareness, self-regulation, motivation, empathy, and social skills—you position yourself as a leader who others respect, trust, and want to follow. You'll not only inspire loyalty and confidence but also create an environment where your team feels seen, heard, and supported. When people feel valued, they're more engaged, innovative, and willing to go above and beyond to achieve shared goals.

But emotional intelligence isn't just about understanding and managing others—it starts with leading yourself. Leadership isn't about suppressing emotions or pretending to be unshakable under pressure. It's about recognizing your own feelings, understanding their impact on your decisions and behavior, and using that awareness to guide your actions with intentionality and composure.

> *Self-awareness makes you a grounded leader. Self-regulation makes you a calm leader. Empathy makes you a compassionate leader. And emotional intelligence makes you an effective leader.*

When you lead with emotional intelligence, you're not just a manager assigning tasks or measuring performance—you're someone who creates deeper connections and fosters an environment where people can thrive. You're showing your team that their well-being matters as much as the results they produce. This human-centered approach doesn't just improve relationships; it drives success, builds resilience, and inspires a shared commitment to the team's goals.

The most impactful leaders don't just manage—they inspire. They challenge their team to grow while providing the emotional safety and support necessary for success. They balance accountability with compassion, firmness with empathy, and results with relationships. Emotional intelligence is the key to unlocking that balance.

As you grow in your leadership journey, reflect regularly on your emotional intelligence. Are you reacting to situations or responding thoughtfully? Are you listening to understand, or simply waiting for your turn to speak? Are you using your influence to uplift others, or letting stress dictate your tone? These questions are essential because emotional intelligence isn't a one-time skill to master—it's a lifelong practice.

Leadership, at its core, is about impact—and emotional intelligence is how you maximize it. By leading with empathy and awareness, you'll not only achieve results but leave a lasting impression on the people you lead. Long after the projects are completed and the goals are met, what your team will remember is how you made them feel.

Lead with emotional intelligence. It's not just the path to success—it's the path to significance.

Chapter 12: Decision-Making in Leadership: Balancing Logic and Intuition

Introduction: The Weight of Decisions

Every day, leaders face decisions that shape their teams, projects, and organizations. Some are small—like assigning tasks for a meeting—while others are monumental, like choosing the direction of a long-term strategy or hiring a key team member. Regardless of the scale, each decision you make contributes to the culture, performance, and success of your team.

But leadership decisions aren't always straightforward. You're often navigating uncertainty, competing priorities, and limited information. Add to this the pressure of balancing logic, data, and strategy with the human side of leadership—emotions, relationships, and intuition—and it's easy to see why decision-making is one of the most challenging aspects of leadership.

Great leaders don't just make decisions—they make informed, thoughtful decisions that align with their values, goals, and the needs of their teams. They balance logic with intuition, speed with thoroughness, and confidence with humility. They're not afraid to own their decisions, learn from mistakes, and adapt when necessary.

In this chapter, we'll explore:

1. The key principles of effective decision-making.
2. How to balance logical analysis and intuition in leadership decisions.
3. Strategies for making decisions under pressure.
4. Techniques for engaging your team in the decision-making process.

Let's uncover the tools and mindset you need to lead decisively in even the most complex situations.

Section 1: The Core Principles of Effective Decision-Making

1. Align Decisions with Your Values and Goals

The best decisions are grounded in your core values and aligned with your long-term goals. As a leader, your decisions set the tone for your team and reflect what you prioritize.

- **How to stay aligned**:
    - When facing a tough decision, ask: *"Does this align with our values as a team or organization?"*
    - Keep your long-term vision in mind and evaluate how the decision supports or detracts from it.

Example: If one of your team's core values is innovation, choosing a riskier but more creative approach to solving a problem may align better than sticking with the status quo.

2. Balance Logic and Intuition

Effective decision-making requires balancing the **logical** and **intuitive** sides of leadership.

- **Logic**: Rely on data, facts, and objective analysis to make well-informed decisions.
- **Intuition**: Trust your instincts and draw on your experience when navigating uncertainty or ambiguity.

Example: When deciding whether to launch a new product, logic might guide you to review market data and customer feedback, while intuition might help you sense whether the timing feels right.

3. Take Ownership of Your Decisions

Leadership means being accountable for your choices, even when the outcome isn't what you expected. Taking ownership builds trust and credibility with your team.

Example: If a decision leads to a missed deadline, avoid blaming others. Instead, say,

"I take responsibility for this outcome, and here's how we'll adjust moving forward."

Section 2: Balancing Logic and Intuition in Decision-Making

1. The Role of Logic

Logical decision-making ensures that your choices are grounded in facts and analysis.

- **Steps for logical decisions**:
    1. Define the problem clearly.
    2. Gather relevant data and insights.
    3. Evaluate potential solutions and their risks.
    4. Make an informed choice based on evidence.

Tip: Use frameworks like cost-benefit analysis or decision matrices to evaluate options objectively.

2. The Role of Intuition

Intuition comes from your experience, expertise, and subconscious pattern recognition. While it shouldn't replace logic, it's a valuable tool for navigating uncertainty.

- **When to trust your gut**:
    - When time is limited, and you need to make a quick decision.
    - When there's no clear data, and you must rely on experience.
    - When your instincts signal that something is off, even if the data looks fine.

Example: A candidate looks great on paper, but your intuition tells you they're not a cultural fit. Balancing logic and intuition might mean revisiting the interview process to explore potential red flags.

3. Balancing Both

The best decisions come from using logic and intuition together.

- Start with logic to gather information and narrow your options.
- Use intuition to evaluate the "intangibles" and make the final call.

Tip: If your intuition conflicts with the data, take a step back and reassess. Ask yourself: *"What might I be overlooking?"*

Section 3: Making Decisions Under Pressure

Leaders often face high-pressure decisions where time is limited, stakes are high, and emotions run strong. Developing strategies to handle these situations is critical.

1. Stay Calm and Focused

Stress clouds judgment, so staying calm is the first step to making sound decisions under pressure.

- **Techniques**:
    - Take a deep breath or pause for a few moments before reacting.

- Break the decision into smaller, more manageable steps.

Example: During a sudden budget cut, instead of panicking, focus on prioritizing essential projects and reevaluating non-critical expenses.

2. Prioritize and Simplify

In high-pressure situations, focus on the most critical decision first. Eliminate unnecessary complexity to maintain clarity.

- **Questions to ask**:
    - *"What's the immediate priority?"*
    - *"What's the simplest path to address this issue effectively?"*

3. Seek Input When Possible

Even in time-sensitive scenarios, consulting your team or peers can provide valuable perspectives and prevent blind spots.

Example: In a crisis, involve key team members in a quick huddle to brainstorm solutions before making a final call.

Section 4: Engaging Your Team in Decision-Making

Great leaders know when to make decisions independently and when to involve their team. Including others in the decision-making process builds trust, ownership, and collaboration.

1. When to Involve Your Team

- When the decision affects the entire team.
- When diverse perspectives can improve the outcome.
- When buy-in is critical for implementation.

2. Techniques for Collaborative Decision-Making

- **Brainstorming sessions**: Generate creative ideas as a group.
- **Consensus-building**: Work toward a decision everyone supports.

- **Voting**: Use democratic methods for lower-stakes decisions.

Tip: Balance collaboration with leadership. If the team is stuck, take the lead in making the final call.

3. Communicate the Decision Clearly

Once a decision is made, communicate it to your team with transparency and clarity.

- **Key elements to include**:
    - The rationale behind the decision.
    - How it aligns with team or organizational goals.
    - Next steps and expectations.

Example: "We've decided to prioritize Project A over Project B for the next quarter because it aligns more closely with our revenue targets. Here's what that means for each of you."

Practical Exercises for Decision-Making

Exercise 1: Decision-Making Self-Assessment

1. Reflect on a recent decision you made.
2. Ask yourself:
    - Did I balance logic and intuition?
    - Was the decision aligned with my values and goals?
    - How did I communicate the decision to my team?

Exercise 2: Practice with Decision-Making Frameworks

1. Use a framework like the Eisenhower Matrix or a cost-benefit analysis for an upcoming decision.
2. Compare the outcome to a decision made without a framework and evaluate the difference.

Exercise 3: Role-Playing Under Pressure

1. Create a high-pressure scenario (e.g., a major project delay or budget cut).

2. Practice staying calm, simplifying the decision, and involving others in the process.

Closing Thought: Decisive Leadership with Clarity and Confidence

Decision-making is at the heart of leadership. Each decision you make, no matter how small, has the potential to build trust, drive results, and move your team closer to its goals. By balancing logic with intuition, engaging your team when appropriate, and maintaining composure under pressure, you'll navigate even the toughest decisions with clarity and confidence.

Great leaders don't aim for perfection—they aim for progress. They understand that not every decision will be flawless, but every decision offers an opportunity to learn and grow. They own their choices, embrace feedback, and adapt when needed.

In the end, leadership isn't about always having the right answers—it's about having the courage to make decisions, the wisdom to adjust when necessary, and the humility to bring others along on the journey.

Lead decisively. Lead thoughtfully. And most importantly, lead with the confidence that every decision you make shapes not only the success of your team but also your growth as a leader.

Chapter 13: Building a High-Performance Team: Unlocking Potential and Driving Results

Introduction: The Leader's Role in Team Success

Behind every successful leader is a high-performing team. As much as leadership is about individual skills and decisions, your true effectiveness is reflected in the team you build, inspire, and guide toward success.

High-performance teams don't happen by chance—they're cultivated. They require more than just hiring skilled individuals; they need a shared vision, trust, clear communication, and an environment where people feel empowered to do their best work. Building such a team is one of the most important and rewarding responsibilities of a leader.

Whether you're managing a small group or leading an entire department, your ability to shape your team's culture and unlock their collective potential determines your success. A high-performing team isn't just about meeting goals—it's about creating a sense of purpose, fostering collaboration, and helping every individual grow.

In this chapter, we'll explore:

1. The characteristics of a high-performance team.
2. Strategies to hire, onboard, and develop top talent.
3. How to build trust, accountability, and alignment within your team.
4. Techniques to sustain performance and foster growth over time.

Great teams are built, not born. Let's dive into the principles and practices that will help you create and lead a team that excels.

Section 1: The Characteristics of a High-Performance Team

High-performing teams share common traits that set them apart from average groups. These characteristics don't just emerge on their own—they require deliberate effort from the leader.

1. Clear Goals and Shared Vision

- **What it looks like**: Everyone on the team understands the mission, goals, and priorities. Each person knows how their role contributes to the team's success.
- **Why it matters**: Clarity provides focus and ensures everyone is working toward the same objectives.

Example: A product development team with a shared goal to launch a customer-focused app by the end of the quarter is more aligned and productive than one with vague or conflicting priorities.

2. Trust and Psychological Safety

- **What it looks like**: Team members feel comfortable speaking up, sharing ideas, and admitting mistakes without fear of judgment or retaliation.
- **Why it matters**: Trust fosters open communication and collaboration, while psychological safety encourages innovation and risk-taking.

Example: A marketing team feels safe brainstorming bold, unconventional campaign ideas because they know their leader values creativity, even if some ideas don't work out.

3. Strong Communication

- **What it looks like**: Team members share information openly, listen actively, and resolve conflicts constructively.

- **Why it matters**: Clear communication reduces misunderstandings, prevents silos, and keeps the team aligned.

Example: A cross-functional team that schedules regular check-ins and uses shared project tools stays informed and avoids duplication of work.

4. Accountability and Ownership

- **What it looks like**: Each team member takes responsibility for their role, delivers on commitments, and supports their peers.
- **Why it matters**: Accountability drives results and ensures that everyone contributes to the team's success.

Example: A sales team member who takes ownership of meeting their individual target inspires others to do the same, creating a culture of accountability.

5. Adaptability and Resilience

- **What it looks like**: The team embraces change, learns from setbacks, and continuously seeks improvement.
- **Why it matters**: In today's fast-changing environment, adaptability is key to staying competitive and achieving long-term success.

Example: A team that quickly pivots to a new strategy after market conditions shift is more likely to succeed than one resistant to change.

Section 2: Hiring and Onboarding for Success

Great teams start with great people. Hiring and onboarding are your first opportunities to set your team up for success.

1. Hiring for Skills and Culture Fit

- Look for candidates who not only have the technical skills but also align with your team's values and culture.

- Ask behavioral interview questions to assess soft skills like communication, adaptability, and teamwork.

  Example: During an interview, ask, "Can you describe a time when you collaborated with a challenging colleague? How did you handle it?"

2. Setting Expectations from Day One

- Provide clear role descriptions and explain how the new hire fits into the team's overall goals.
- Share your leadership style and expectations for communication, feedback, and accountability.

  Tip: Use the first 90 days to establish trust and help new team members feel supported as they ramp up.

3. Fostering Connection During Onboarding

- Pair new hires with mentors or "buddies" to help them integrate into the team.

- Schedule one-on-one meetings to check in on their progress and address any challenges.

Example: A buddy system where a veteran team member helps onboard a new hire accelerates their understanding of team dynamics and culture.

Section 3: Building Trust, Accountability, and Alignment

1. Create a Culture of Trust

- **How to build trust**:
    - Be transparent in your communication.
    - Follow through on commitments.
    - Show vulnerability by admitting mistakes.

Tip: Regularly recognize your team's contributions to demonstrate your trust in their abilities.

2. Foster Accountability

- **How to foster accountability**:
    - Set clear expectations for individual and team performance.
    - Use regular check-ins to track progress and address challenges.
    - Celebrate successes and address missed commitments constructively.

Example: During a team meeting, review each member's progress on their goals to create a sense of shared accountability.

3. Align Team Efforts with Organizational Goals

- Connect the team's work to the bigger picture by regularly revisiting how their efforts support the organization's mission.

Tip: Use visuals, like dashboards or scorecards, to track and communicate progress toward goals.

Section 4: Sustaining High Performance Over Time

Building a high-performance team isn't a one-time effort—it requires ongoing care and attention.

1. Invest in Professional Development

- Provide opportunities for training, mentorship, and skill-building to keep your team engaged and growing.

    Example: Offer workshops or certifications for team members who want to develop leadership or technical skills.

2. Recognize and Reward Contributions

- Celebrate wins, both big and small, to boost morale and reinforce positive behaviors.

    Tip: Tailor recognition to individual preferences—some team members prefer public praise, while others appreciate private acknowledgment.

3. Conduct Regular Team Reviews

- Reflect on what's working and what's not. Encourage open dialogue about challenges and opportunities for improvement.

Example: At the end of each quarter, hold a retrospective meeting to discuss lessons learned and set goals for the next quarter.

Practical Exercises for Building High-Performance Teams

Exercise 1: Team Values Assessment

- Have your team define the top three values that guide their work.
- Discuss how these values align with your goals and how they can be reinforced daily.

Exercise 2: Building Psychological Safety

- During a team meeting, ask:
    - *"What's one thing we can do to make this team a safer space for sharing ideas?"*
    - *"What's one thing we should stop doing to improve trust?"*

Exercise 3: Quarterly Team Review

- Use these prompts to evaluate your team's performance:
    - What are we doing well as a team?
    - Where can we improve?
    - What's one thing we'll commit to doing differently next quarter?

Section 5: The Stages of Team Development

Building a high-performance team is a journey that follows specific stages of growth. Dr. Bruce Tuckman's **Stages of Team Development**—*Forming, Storming, Norming, and Performing*—provide a framework for understanding this process. Each stage presents unique challenges and opportunities for leaders.

1. Forming

- **What happens**: The team comes together, and members focus on understanding their roles and goals. There's excitement but also uncertainty.
- **Leader's role**: Provide clear direction, set expectations, and establish trust.

Example: During a project kickoff, outline the team's goals, assign roles, and set the tone for collaboration.

2. Storming

- **What happens**: Conflicts and growing pains arise as team members test boundaries and navigate differences.
- **Leader's role**: Facilitate open communication, resolve conflicts, and reinforce shared goals.

Tip: During this phase, hold regular check-ins to address concerns and keep the team aligned.

3. Norming

- **What happens**: The team develops stronger relationships and establishes norms for working together effectively.
- **Leader's role**: Strengthen trust, foster collaboration, and encourage shared ownership of success.

Example: Celebrate small wins to reinforce teamwork and build momentum.

4. Performing

- **What happens**: The team operates at a high level of efficiency, collaboration, and trust. They take ownership of their roles and achieve results.
- **Leader's role**: Provide support, remove roadblocks, and challenge the team to continue growing.

Tip: Even in this phase, stay attentive to team dynamics to prevent complacency or burnout.

Section 6: Tools for Building High-Performance Teams

1. Team Charters

A **team charter** is a document that outlines the team's mission, goals, roles, and rules for collaboration. It sets a foundation for accountability and alignment.

- **What to include**:
    - Mission statement
    - Key goals and deliverables
    - Roles and responsibilities
    - Communication norms and decision-making processes

    Tip: Create the charter collaboratively during the "Forming" stage to ensure buy-in from all team members.

2. The RACI Matrix

A **RACI matrix** clarifies who is Responsible, Accountable, Consulted, and Informed for each task or decision.

- **How it helps**: Prevents misunderstandings and ensures everyone knows their role in the project.
- **Example RACI Assignment**:
    - *Responsible*: The person doing the work.
    - *Accountable*: The person who owns the outcome.
    - *Consulted*: People whose input is needed.
    - *Informed*: People who need to be kept updated.

3. Feedback Loops

Regular feedback keeps the team on track and fosters continuous improvement.

- **How to implement**:
    - Conduct weekly check-ins.
    - Hold retrospectives after completing major projects.

- Use anonymous surveys to gather honest input.

Example: After a product launch, hold a team retrospective to discuss what worked, what didn't, and how to improve next time.

Section 6: The Role of Diversity in High-Performance Teams

1. Why Diversity Matters

Diverse teams bring a wider range of perspectives, ideas, and problem-solving approaches, making them more innovative and adaptable.

- **Research insight**: Studies show that diverse teams outperform homogeneous ones, particularly on complex tasks.

2. How to Foster Diversity

- **Hire for diversity**: Expand your talent pool by reaching out to underrepresented groups.

- **Create an inclusive culture**: Ensure all voices are heard, respected, and valued.
- **Leverage differences**: Use the team's varied perspectives to tackle challenges creatively.

Example: During brainstorming sessions, encourage quieter team members to share their ideas, ensuring everyone contributes.

Section 7: Overcoming Common Team Challenges

1. Resolving Conflict

- **How to approach it**:
    1. Address conflicts early before they escalate.
    2. Focus on behaviors, not personalities.
    3. Facilitate open dialogue to find common ground.

Example: If two team members clash over responsibilities, clarify their roles and ensure they understand how their efforts contribute to the larger goal.

2. Breaking Down Silos

Silos occur when teams or departments fail to communicate effectively, leading to duplication of effort or conflicting priorities.

- **How to fix it:**
    - Schedule cross-functional meetings.
    - Use shared project management tools to improve transparency.

    Example: A sales and marketing team can hold weekly alignment meetings to coordinate messaging and strategies.

3. Reigniting Engagement

Low engagement can hurt morale and productivity.

- **How to boost engagement:**
    - Celebrate wins, no matter how small.
    - Reconnect the team to the "why" behind their work.

- Provide growth opportunities through training or stretch assignments.

Section 8: Vision and Purpose in Teams

A strong team vision inspires motivation and commitment.

1. Crafting a Team Vision

- Collaborate with your team to define a vision that aligns with the organization's mission.
- Make it specific, inspiring, and actionable.

Example: A customer service team's vision could be: "To deliver world-class support that turns every customer interaction into a memorable experience."

2. Keeping the Vision Alive

- Revisit the vision regularly during meetings and goal-setting sessions.
- Use it to guide decisions and priorities.

Tip: Create a visual representation of the team's vision and display it prominently in the office or virtual workspace.

Section 9: Real-World Case Studies

Case Study 1: Transforming a Struggling Team

A newly promoted manager inherits a disengaged and underperforming team. By rebuilding trust, clarifying goals, and fostering accountability, they turn the team into a top performer within a year.

Key Takeaway: Consistent communication, transparency, and celebrating small wins can transform team dynamics.

Case Study 2: A Diverse Team Drives Innovation

A tech company forms a cross-functional team with members from engineering, marketing, and customer support to design a new product. By leveraging their diverse perspectives, they create a product that exceeds market expectations.

Key Takeaway: Diversity fuels innovation when paired with strong collaboration and inclusive leadership.

Closing Thought: High-Performance Leadership

Great leaders understand that their success is only as strong as the team they lead. Building a high-performance team isn't about micromanaging or pushing for results at all costs—it's about fostering an environment where people feel inspired, supported, and empowered to reach their full potential.

When you focus on trust, accountability, and alignment, you create the conditions for your team to thrive. By investing in their growth, celebrating their contributions, and adapting to new challenges, you'll build a team that not only meets goals but exceeds them.

Leadership is about people, and people are at their best when they feel valued, challenged, and connected to a shared purpose. Commit to building a high-performance team—not just for what they can achieve, but for the impact they can create together.

Chapter 15: Sustaining Leadership Growth: A Commitment to Continuous Improvement

Introduction: Leadership is a Journey, Not a Destination

Leadership isn't a title or a final achievement—it's an ongoing journey of growth, learning, and self-reflection. Even the most accomplished leaders recognize that they are never finished improving. The best leaders continuously ask themselves, *"How can I be better tomorrow than I am today?"*

In today's fast-paced, ever-changing world, stagnation is not an option. Markets shift, teams evolve, and challenges become more complex. To stay effective, you must adapt, learn, and refine your leadership approach. Sustaining leadership growth isn't just about acquiring new skills—it's about developing the mindset, habits, and resilience needed to lead with excellence over the long term.

This chapter will explore how to:

1. Cultivate a mindset of continuous learning and curiosity.
2. Seek feedback and use it as a tool for growth.
3. Balance personal development with leadership responsibilities.
4. Stay adaptable and resilient in the face of change.

Great leaders don't stop growing because they understand this truth: leadership isn't something you master—it's something you live.

Section 1: Embracing a Growth Mindset

A **growth mindset**, a term popularized by psychologist Carol Dweck, is the belief that skills and abilities can be developed through effort, learning, and perseverance. Leaders with a growth mindset view challenges as opportunities, setbacks as lessons, and success as a journey rather than a destination.

1. The Difference Between Fixed and Growth Mindsets

- **Fixed mindset**: Believes that leadership ability is innate and unchangeable.
- **Growth mindset**: Sees leadership as a skill that can be cultivated through learning and experience.

Example: A leader with a growth mindset views critical feedback as an opportunity to improve, while one with a fixed mindset may see it as a personal attack.

2. How to Cultivate a Growth Mindset

- **Reframe challenges**: Instead of asking, *"Why is this so hard?"* ask, *"What can I learn from this?"*
- **Celebrate progress, not just results**: Focus on the journey, not just the outcome.

- **Learn from mistakes**: See failures as stepping stones to improvement.

Tip: At the end of each week, reflect on one challenge you faced and write down what it taught you about yourself or your leadership.

Section 2: Seeking Feedback as a Tool for Growth

Great leaders understand that feedback is a gift. It provides insights into blind spots, highlights areas for improvement, and accelerates personal and professional development.

1. Why Feedback Matters

Feedback helps you:

- Gain clarity on how your actions are perceived.
- Identify areas for growth.
- Build stronger relationships by showing humility and openness.

Example: A leader who regularly seeks feedback from their team fosters trust and sets an example of continuous learning.

2. How to Ask for Feedback

- **Be proactive**: Don't wait for annual reviews or performance evaluations.
- **Ask specific questions**:
    - "What's one thing I could do better to support you?"
    - "How can I improve my communication style?"
- **Follow up**: Show that you've taken feedback seriously by acting on it and sharing your progress.

3. Creating a Feedback Loop

Encourage ongoing feedback by building a culture of open communication within your team.

- **How to create a feedback loop**:

- Regularly ask for feedback during one-on-ones or team meetings.
- Provide feedback to your team in a constructive and consistent manner.

Section 3: Balancing Personal Development with Leadership Responsibilities

As a leader, it's easy to put your team and organization first, leaving little time for your own growth. However, personal development is not a luxury—it's a necessity.

1. Prioritize Time for Learning

Make personal development a non-negotiable part of your schedule.

- **How to prioritize learning**:
    - Dedicate at least 1–2 hours per week to reading, attending webinars, or exploring new ideas.
    - Block time in your calendar for personal reflection or professional development.

Tip: Treat personal development as an investment in your leadership effectiveness, not as an optional task.

2. Learn from Others

Great leaders don't grow in isolation—they learn from peers, mentors, and role models.

- **How to learn from others**:
    - Seek out mentors who can offer guidance and wisdom.
    - Build a network of fellow leaders to share challenges and best practices.
    - Observe and emulate the leadership traits you admire in others.

Example: Join a leadership peer group or mastermind to gain fresh perspectives and accountability.

3. Protect Your Energy

Sustained growth requires energy and focus. Prioritize self-care to avoid burnout and stay at your best.

- **Strategies for protecting your energy**:
  - Set boundaries between work and personal time.
  - Incorporate mindfulness practices like meditation or journaling.
  - Take regular breaks to recharge.

Tip: Remember, you can't pour from an empty cup—take care of yourself to take care of others.

Section 4: Staying Adaptable and Resilient

Leadership is rarely linear. The ability to adapt and remain resilient in the face of change and setbacks is essential for sustaining growth.

1. Embrace Change as an Opportunity

View change as a chance to grow and evolve.

- **How to stay adaptable**:
    - Stay curious and open to new ideas.
    - Develop contingency plans to prepare for uncertainty.
    - Practice flexibility by experimenting with different approaches to problem-solving.

2. Build Resilience Through Reflection

Resilience isn't about avoiding challenges—it's about bouncing back stronger.

- **How to build resilience**:
    - Reflect on past challenges and how you overcame them.
    - Focus on what you can control, rather than what you can't.
    - Maintain a positive outlook by practicing gratitude and celebrating small wins.

Example: After a major setback, a resilient leader gathers their team, acknowledges the difficulty, and refocuses on the next steps to move forward.

Practical Exercises for Sustaining Leadership Growth

Exercise 1: Weekly Growth Reflection

At the end of each week, reflect on:

1. What leadership challenges did I face?
2. What did I learn from them?
3. What will I do differently next time?

Exercise 2: 360-Degree Feedback Survey

1. Ask your team, peers, and supervisors for feedback on your leadership.
2. Use a mix of open-ended questions and ratings to gather insights.
3. Identify one area for improvement and create an action plan to address it.

Exercise 3: Personal Development Plan

1. Identify one leadership skill you want to improve (e.g., decision-making, delegation, or conflict resolution).
2. Set a specific, measurable goal for developing that skill.
3. Outline steps to achieve the goal (e.g., books to read, courses to take, or mentors to consult).

Closing Thought: Leadership as a Lifelong Commitment

Leadership isn't a sprint—it's a marathon. It's not about reaching a destination but about continuously evolving to meet the demands of an ever-changing world. The best leaders understand that growth isn't optional; it's essential.

By embracing a growth mindset, seeking feedback, and investing in your personal development, you demonstrate the humility and dedication that great leadership requires. You also set an example for your team, showing them that continuous improvement is not just a principle but a way of life.

Remember, the challenges you face today are shaping the leader you'll become tomorrow. With every setback, you gain resilience. With every lesson, you gain wisdom. And with every effort to grow, you gain the ability to lead with greater clarity, empathy, and impact.

Leadership is a journey, and the path to greatness is paved with curiosity, reflection, and a relentless commitment to becoming the best version of yourself. Keep learning, keep adapting, and keep leading. The future of your leadership is limitless.

Chapter 16: Leaving a Legacy: The Impact of Great Leadership

Introduction: Leadership That Endures

At its core, leadership is about more than just achieving goals, hitting metrics, or building high-performing teams. While these accomplishments are important, they are often temporary—bound to the moment and the circumstances in which they occur. What truly sets great leaders apart is their ability to create a lasting impact—a legacy.

A leadership legacy isn't measured by how many tasks you completed or awards you won; it's defined by the values you instilled, the culture you cultivated, and the lives you influenced along the way. It's what people remember about you after you're gone—not just as a leader, but as a person. Did you empower others to grow? Did you create an environment where people thrived? Did you inspire a sense of purpose that transcended your time in the role?

Leadership is temporary, but its ripple effects can be permanent. The culture you create, the systems you build, and the people you mentor have the potential to continue shaping the organization, your industry, and even the broader community for years to come. A legacy isn't about being remembered for your achievements; it's about ensuring your impact lives on in the success and growth of others.

In this chapter, we will explore how to lead with a legacy mindset. This means thinking beyond the day-to-day challenges and focusing on the long-term effects of your actions. It's about leading with intention—recognizing that every decision you make, every conversation you have, and every value you model contributes to the mark you leave behind.

This chapter will guide you through:

1. **Defining your personal leadership legacy**: What do you want to stand for as a leader, and how do you want to be remembered?
2. **Building a culture that lasts**: How can you create a team environment where values, trust, and collaboration outlive your tenure?
3. **Empowering others to lead**: How can you mentor and develop future leaders who will carry your vision forward?
4. **Aligning daily actions with long-term goals**: How do you ensure that your everyday decisions support your legacy?

A leadership legacy isn't built overnight. It's shaped over time, through consistent actions and decisions that reflect your values and your vision. As you read this chapter, take a moment to step back from the urgency of today's tasks and ask yourself:

- What kind of leader do I want to be?
- How do I want my leadership to be remembered?

- What impact do I want to leave on the people and organizations I've touched?

Your answers to these questions will serve as your compass, guiding you toward a legacy that endures.

Leadership is not just about leading in the moment—it's about leading beyond yourself. Let's explore how to create a legacy that inspires, uplifts, and endures.

Section 1: Defining Your Leadership Legacy

1. What is a Leadership Legacy?

A leadership legacy is the lasting impact of your values, actions, and decisions on the people and organizations you've led.

- **Examples of legacies**:
    - A team culture that prioritizes collaboration and innovation.
    - Processes or systems that improve efficiency and remain in place after your departure.

- People you've mentored who go on to lead successfully in their own right.

2. Reflecting on the Legacy You Want to Leave

Take time to reflect on how you want to be remembered as a leader.

- **Questions to ask yourself**:
  - What values do I want my team to embody even after I'm gone?
  - How do I want my team to describe my leadership?
  - What contributions do I want to make to my organization and industry?

Tip: Think about a leader you admire and the legacy they left. Use their example to clarify your own aspirations.

3. Aligning Legacy with Values

Your legacy is rooted in your values. Ensure your daily actions reflect the principles you want to be known for.

- **Examples of legacy values**:
    - Integrity: Building trust by always doing the right thing.
    - Empowerment: Helping others realize their potential.
    - Vision: Creating a clear and inspiring path forward.

Section 2: Building a Culture That Outlasts You

1. The Power of Team Culture

Culture isn't just what you say—it's what you do. The values, behaviors, and norms you cultivate as a leader form the foundation of your legacy.

- **How to build a strong culture**:
    - Model the behaviors you want to see in your team.
    - Create rituals and traditions that reinforce team values.

- Regularly communicate the "why" behind your team's work to keep them aligned with the vision.

Example: A leader who consistently prioritizes collaboration and respect leaves behind a culture where people continue to support one another long after they've moved on.

2. Systems and Processes that Endure

Legacy isn't just about people—it's also about creating systems and processes that make work easier and more effective.

- **How to create lasting systems**:
    - Document best practices and workflows.
    - Streamline processes to ensure efficiency.
    - Train team members to use and sustain these systems effectively.

Example: A leader who implements a project management framework leaves the team with tools to maintain productivity even in their absence.

3. Championing a Vision

A compelling vision unites people and inspires them to continue striving for excellence.

- **How to champion your vision:**
    - Share it regularly and passionately.
    - Align team goals and decisions with the vision.
    - Celebrate milestones that bring the team closer to achieving it.

Tip: A vision doesn't end with one leader—it becomes part of the team's identity when consistently reinforced.

Section 3: Mentoring Future Leaders

1. The Multiplier Effect of Leadership

The best leaders don't just lead—they create more leaders. Mentorship amplifies your impact by preparing others to step into leadership roles and continue your work.

- **Why mentorship matters**:
    - It ensures continuity when leadership transitions occur.
    - It strengthens your team by empowering individuals to grow.
    - It builds your legacy through the success of those you've mentored.

2. How to Mentor Effectively

- **Be intentional**: Identify high-potential team members and invest time in their development.
- **Provide guidance and feedback**: Share lessons from your experience while encouraging them to find their own style.
- **Offer opportunities**: Give mentees chances to lead projects or make decisions.

Example: A manager mentors a junior team member by including them in strategic planning meetings, providing constructive feedback, and gradually increasing their responsibilities.

3. Succession Planning

One of the most practical ways to leave a legacy is to prepare the next generation of leaders.

- **Steps for succession planning**:
    - Identify key roles and the skills required for them.
    - Develop a pipeline of potential successors through training and development.
    - Gradually transition responsibilities to ensure a smooth handoff.

Tip: Succession planning isn't about replacing yourself—it's about ensuring the team thrives without you.

Section 4: Aligning Daily Actions with Long-Term Impact

1. Leading with Intention

Every decision you make and every interaction you have shapes your legacy. Be intentional about how you spend your time and energy.

- **Questions to guide your actions**:
    - Does this decision align with my values?
    - How will this action impact my team in the long run?

2. Celebrating Small Wins

Legacy isn't built in a single moment—it's the result of consistent effort over time. Celebrate progress along the way to reinforce your vision and values.

> *Example*: Recognize team members who embody the culture you're building, such as collaboration, creativity, or resilience.

3. Measuring Your Impact

Take time to reflect on the impact you're making as a leader.

- **How to measure your legacy:**
    - Look at the culture and systems you've built.
    - Consider the growth of the people you've mentored.
    - Gather feedback from your team on how your leadership has influenced them.

Practical Exercises for Leaving a Legacy

Exercise 1: Legacy Reflection

Write down how you want to be remembered as a leader.

- What values do you want to be known for?
- What impact do you want to leave on your team or organization?
- What steps can you take now to align your actions with your legacy?

Exercise 2: Team Vision Workshop

Hold a workshop with your team to define or revisit the team's vision and values.

- Discuss how these values align with the broader organizational mission.
- Identify ways to bring these values to life in daily work.

Exercise 3: Mentorship Plan

Create a mentorship plan for one or two team members.

- Identify their strengths and areas for growth.
- Outline specific opportunities to support their development over the next 6–12 months.

Closing Thought: Leading Beyond Yourself

Leadership is temporary, but its impact can last forever. The goals you achieve, the teams you build, and the challenges you overcome are important, but they are just one part of the story. What truly defines your leadership is the legacy you leave behind—the culture, systems, and people who carry your influence forward.

Your leadership legacy is built through the values you uphold, the trust you foster, and the example you set for others. Every decision you make and every interaction you have shapes the mark you leave—not just on your team or organization, but on the lives of the individuals you lead. Long after you've stepped away from your role, your impact will echo in the confidence you've instilled in others, the lessons you've taught, and the inspiration you've provided.

To leave a meaningful legacy, you must focus on more than just results—you must focus on people. A true legacy isn't measured in accolades or financial outcomes; it's measured in the growth and empowerment of those you've mentored, the cultures you've built, and the systems you've created that enable future success. The greatest leaders don't just drive short-term wins; they create lasting change by investing in others, sharing their wisdom, and building a foundation for sustained excellence.

Leadership Is About Legacy, Not Longevity

Your legacy is not defined by how long you held a position or the authority you commanded. Instead, it's defined by the consistency of your actions, the strength of your character, and the extent to which you've enabled others to grow. Leadership is not about creating followers—it's about developing other leaders.

By mentoring and empowering others, you multiply your impact. The leaders you develop will carry your lessons forward, applying them in their own unique ways and building legacies of their own. This multiplier effect is what separates transactional leadership from transformational leadership.

Leaving a Culture, Not Just a Role

When you approach leadership with a legacy mindset, you focus on creating systems, processes, and a culture that persist beyond your time in the role. A strong team culture based on trust, respect, and collaboration doesn't just survive—it thrives—long after a leader has moved on.

Consider this: If you were to leave your role tomorrow, what would remain? Would the team you've built feel empowered to continue moving forward, or would they struggle in your absence? A great legacy ensures continuity and strength, allowing others to carry the torch without losing sight of the vision.

Every Day is a Step Toward Your Legacy

Leadership legacy is not something you craft in your final days in a role—it's something you build every day through your actions, decisions, and interactions. Every moment you spend investing in your team, upholding your values, and championing your vision contributes to the story you'll leave behind.

To ensure your daily actions align with the legacy you want to leave, ask yourself:

- Am I making decisions today that reflect my long-term values?
- Am I empowering others to grow and succeed?
- Am I modeling the kind of behavior I want to see in the organization after I'm gone?

Your Leadership Ripple Effect

Great leaders create ripples that extend far beyond their immediate reach. The systems you implement, the culture you cultivate, and the people you mentor are all part of that ripple effect. They carry your influence into new teams, new roles, and even new industries. Your leadership legacy isn't limited to one moment in time—it's a lasting impact that shapes future generations.

Think of the leaders who have inspired you. Chances are, their influence didn't end with their immediate accomplishments. Their lessons and values continue to guide and motivate you, even if they're no longer present. This is the power of a leadership legacy—it transcends time, touching lives in ways you may never fully realize.

A Call to Action: Build Your Legacy Now

The question is not whether you'll leave a legacy—you will. The question is what kind of legacy you'll leave. Will it be one of empowerment, trust, and progress? Or will it be a legacy of missed opportunities, stagnant culture, and unfulfilled potential?

The choice is yours, and it begins today.

- Mentor someone who shows potential but lacks confidence.
- Create a system or process that simplifies work for future teams.
- Model values like integrity, empathy, and resilience in every decision you make.
- Foster a team culture where people feel safe, supported, and inspired to grow.

By leading with intention, you ensure that your legacy will outlast your tenure. Long after your team has moved on to new challenges and opportunities, your influence will live on in the people, systems, and culture you've shaped.

Leadership is not about what you accomplish during your time—it's about what you leave behind when your time is over. Build a legacy that inspires, uplifts, and empowers others to achieve greatness.

Because at the end of the day, the greatest leaders don't just create success—they create significance.

Conclusion: The Leadership Journey

Leadership is not a destination—it's a journey of growth, self-discovery, and impact. From the moment you first step into a leadership role to the time you pass the torch, the path you walk as a leader will shape not only your own development but the lives and careers of those you lead.

This book has taken you through the key phases of leadership, from transitioning into a management role to building high-performance teams, navigating challenges, and leaving a lasting legacy. Along the way, you've explored essential skills like emotional intelligence, time management, decision-making, and leading through change. But leadership isn't about mastering these skills once and moving on. It's about continually refining and applying them as you face new challenges, opportunities, and contexts.

Reflecting on Your Leadership Growth

Think back to when you first began your leadership journey. What motivated you to lead? Perhaps it was the desire to make a difference, a passion for solving problems, or a drive to inspire others. Over time, your role may have evolved, but your purpose remains central: to guide, empower, and create a positive impact.

As you reflect on your journey so far, ask yourself:

- How have I grown as a leader?
- What lessons have I learned from my successes and failures?
- How has my leadership positively influenced those around me?

These questions are not only a chance to appreciate how far you've come but also an invitation to focus on where you want to go next.

The Future of Leadership: Your Next Steps

Leadership is never static. As organizations, industries, and teams evolve, so must you. Here are three commitments to carry forward as you continue to grow:

1. Commit to Lifelong Learning

Leadership isn't something you "master"—it's a skillset and mindset that requires constant growth. Commit to staying curious, seeking feedback, and learning from every experience.

> *Tip*: Make personal development a habit, whether it's reading leadership books, attending workshops, or reflecting on your challenges and achievements.

2. Lead with Purpose and Values

The most enduring leaders are guided by a sense of purpose and a strong set of values. These principles act as your compass, helping you navigate uncertainty and make decisions that align with your vision for leadership.

> *Tip*: Revisit your purpose regularly and ensure your actions reflect the values you want to embody.

3. Focus on Building Others Up

The greatest leaders measure their success not by what they accomplish but by the success of those they've influenced. By mentoring, empowering, and creating opportunities for others, you amplify your impact and leave a legacy that endures.

> *Tip*: Ask yourself, *"What can I do today to help someone else grow?"*

The Leader You've Become

Leadership is a privilege. It's an opportunity to shape lives, inspire progress, and leave a lasting mark on the world around you. As you continue your leadership journey, remember that every decision, every conversation, and every challenge is a chance to grow and make an impact.

This book is not the end of your development as a leader—it's a starting point. The tools, strategies, and insights you've gained here are meant to guide you, but your journey is uniquely yours.

So, lead with intention. Lead with empathy. And most importantly, lead with the knowledge that your leadership matters.

> *"The best way to predict the future is to create it." – Peter Drucker*

You are not just managing tasks or overseeing teams—you are shaping futures. The impact you make as a leader will ripple far beyond what you can see today. Embrace the responsibility, the challenges, and the opportunities. And above all, continue to grow, learn, and lead boldly.

Leadership: A Lifelong Journey

Leadership is not a title, a position, or a milestone—it's a continuous journey. From the moment you first stepped into a leadership role, your path has been one of growth, challenge, and transformation. As a leader, you shape not only the direction of your team and organization but also the lives of those you influence.

This book has been a guide for the key phases of your leadership evolution—from transitioning into management, building trust and accountability, and navigating change to empowering others, making impactful decisions, and leaving a lasting legacy. But your journey doesn't stop here.

Leadership is an ever-evolving practice. Each new challenge, opportunity, and experience offers a chance to refine your skills, deepen your self-awareness, and expand your impact. True leadership is about staying open to growth, no matter how far you've come.

Reflecting on Your Leadership Growth

Before you look ahead to the next steps in your journey, take a moment to reflect on how far you've already come.

Questions for Reflection

1. **How have I grown?**
   - Think about the challenges you've overcome and the lessons you've learned.
2. **Who have I impacted?**
   - Consider the people you've mentored, supported, and inspired along the way.
3. **What have I achieved?**
   - Reflect on the teams you've built, the goals you've reached, and the culture you've created.
4. **Where can I improve?**
   - Identify the areas where you still have room to grow and explore new opportunities for development.

Tip: Journaling your thoughts can help clarify your leadership strengths and areas for growth.

Leadership is About Progress, Not Perfection

No leader is perfect, and that's okay. Leadership isn't about flawless execution; it's about progress, humility, and the willingness to learn from every success and setback. By embracing a mindset of continuous improvement, you ensure that every step forward is a step toward becoming the leader you aspire to be.

The Future of Leadership: Your Next Steps

1. Commit to Lifelong Learning

The best leaders never stop learning. They read, listen, and reflect. They actively seek out new experiences and diverse perspectives to challenge their thinking and expand their horizons.

- **How to stay committed**:
    - Read one leadership book per quarter or follow a podcast that inspires you.
    - Attend workshops or conferences to stay up-to-date on trends and best practices.
    - Regularly seek feedback from peers, mentors, and your team to uncover blind spots.

Tip: Keep a personal leadership journal where you jot down lessons learned, insights gained, and areas to explore further.

2. Lead with Purpose and Values

Purpose-driven leadership is powerful because it gives your decisions and actions meaning beyond the day-to-day. Your values serve as the compass that guides you through uncertainty, helping you stay true to what matters most.

- **How to lead with purpose**:
    - Reflect on your "why" as a leader. Why do you lead, and what impact do you want to make?
    - Revisit your values regularly and ensure your actions align with them.
    - Inspire your team by sharing your vision and connecting their work to a greater purpose.

Example: If your purpose is to empower others, ensure your leadership style prioritizes mentoring, coaching, and creating opportunities for growth.

3. Focus on Building Others Up

The mark of a great leader isn't just in their own success—it's in the success of those they've empowered. By mentoring, coaching, and developing future leaders, you multiply your impact and ensure your influence extends far beyond your time in any one role.

- **How to build others up**:
    - Identify team members with leadership potential and provide opportunities for them to grow.
    - Share your knowledge and experiences through regular coaching sessions.
    - Encourage autonomy by delegating meaningful responsibilities and trusting your team to rise to the occasion.

Tip: Celebrate your team's achievements as a reflection of your leadership legacy.

Resources for Continued Leadership Growth

Books

1. *Dare to Lead* by Brené Brown – A guide to leading with courage, vulnerability, and authenticity.
2. *Mindset* by Carol Dweck – The psychology behind embracing challenges and cultivating a growth mindset.
3. *The 7 Habits of Highly Effective People* by Stephen Covey – Timeless principles for personal and professional growth.
4. *Leaders Eat Last* by Simon Sinek – How great leaders create trust and foster a culture of collaboration.

Podcasts

1. *The Knowledge Project* – Insights on decision-making, leadership, and personal development.

2. *Coaching for Leaders* – Practical strategies for becoming a more effective and thoughtful leader.
3. *WorkLife with Adam Grant* – Exploring how to create meaningful, productive work environments.

Assessment Tools

1. **StrengthsFinder 2.0**: Identify your core leadership strengths.
2. **360-Degree Feedback**: Gather insights from peers, subordinates, and supervisors to better understand your impact.
3. **DISC Assessment**: Understand your behavioral tendencies and how they influence your leadership style.

Final Exercise: Craft Your Leadership Vision

To close this book and begin the next phase of your leadership journey, create a written vision for the leader you aspire to be.

Prompt for Your Vision Statement

- **Values**: What core principles will guide your leadership?
- **Impact**: How do you want to positively influence your team, organization, or industry?
- **Legacy**: What do you want people to say about your leadership after you've moved on?

Example Vision Statement:
"I want to be a leader who inspires trust, fosters growth, and creates a culture of collaboration and innovation. My legacy will be defined by the people I've empowered and the systems I've built to ensure their long-term success."

Final Words: Leadership That Inspires and Endures

As you close this book, remember that leadership is a privilege. It's an opportunity to shape the future—not just through the results you deliver but through the lives you touch and the values you uphold.

Your leadership matters. It matters to your team, your organization, and the people who look to you for guidance and inspiration. Every day, you have the chance to make an impact—whether it's empowering someone to grow, solving a complex problem, or modeling integrity in a difficult situation.

The greatest leaders are not remembered for their titles or accolades—they're remembered for the difference they made in the lives of others. As you continue your leadership journey, lead with courage, empathy, and purpose. Focus on growth, inspire those around you, and leave a legacy that endures.

Leadership is not a final destination—it's a lifelong commitment. The future of your leadership is unwritten, and its possibilities are limitless.

Go forward boldly, lead with intention, and make your leadership journey one that inspires others to lead, grow, and thrive.

Index

Part 1: The Transition to Leadership

1. **From Peer to Leader**
   - Understanding the Challenges of Leadership
   - Navigating Role Changes
   - Establishing Authority Without Alienating
   - Building Trust and Credibility
2. **Strengthening Relationships in Leadership**
   - Shifting Dynamics with Former Peers
   - Cultivating Professional Boundaries
   - Strengthening New Relationships
   - Leading with Empathy
3. **Understanding Leadership Styles**
   - Common Leadership Styles
   - Discovering Your Leadership Style
   - Adapting Your Style to Your Team's Needs

- The Role of Flexibility in Leadership
4. **Managing Up**
    - Building a Strong Relationship with Your Boss
    - Communicating Upward Effectively
    - Anticipating Needs and Prioritizing Goals
    - Navigating Misalignment and Conflict

Part 2: Skills for Effective Leadership

5. **Time Management for Leaders**
    - Balancing Priorities in a Demanding Role
    - Delegation as a Time-Management Tool
    - Strategic Planning and Focus
    - Avoiding Burnout as a Leader
6. **Decision-Making in Leadership**
    - The Role of Logic and Intuition
    - Making Decisions Under Pressure
    - Engaging the Team in Decisions
    - Owning Outcomes and Learning from Mistakes
7. **Emotional Intelligence in Leadership**
    - The Five Pillars of Emotional Intelligence

- Managing Emotions Effectively
- Building Stronger Relationships with Empathy
- Handling Emotional Conflict in the Workplace

Part 3: Building High-Performing Teams

8. **Building a High-Performance Team**
   - Characteristics of Successful Teams
   - Hiring and Onboarding for Success
   - Building Trust and Accountability
   - Sustaining Team Growth and Performance

9. **Leading Through Change**
   - The Emotional Impact of Change on Teams
   - Communicating Change Effectively
   - Leading with Empathy in Uncertain Times
   - Building Resilience and Adaptability

Part 4: Legacy and Leadership Longevity

10. **Sustaining Leadership Growth**
    - Embracing a Growth Mindset
    - Seeking Feedback for Improvement
    - Balancing Personal Development with Team Needs
    - Staying Resilient and Adaptable
11. **Leaving a Leadership Legacy**
    - Defining the Legacy You Want to Leave
    - Building a Culture That Outlasts You
    - Mentoring and Developing Future Leaders
    - Aligning Your Daily Actions with Your Long-Term Impact